I0137459

On the Planting of Churches

Biblical Principles in the Early Church

On the Planting of Churches

Biblical Principles in the Early Church

William H Jones

ChiRho Communications
Toronto
(wmhjones9@gmail.com)

On the Planting of Churches:
Biblical Principles in the Early Church
William H. Jones.
Copyright © 2010 All rights reserved.
Cover photo of Athens Acropolis
by **William H. Jones**
(wmhjones@gmailcom)

Scripture used in this book is taken from The New International Version, Copyright © 1973, 1978, and 1984 by Biblia, Inc. All rights reserved worldwide. Used by permission.
ISBN 978-0-929081-21-2

Table of Contents

Biblical Competence: Theological Maturity
and Understanding
A Belief in Mission Partnership

B. Human Qualities

A Sense of Urgency: A Possession of
Patience
A Commitment to Conclusions
An Acceptance of Reality
A Sense of Self-Understanding
An Ability to Trust One's Instincts
An Appraisal of Others' Strengths and a
Willingness to Delegate
A Loyalty of Permanence
Follow-up and Remedial Ministry
A Good Measure of Hard Work

Summary

ON THE PLANTING OF CHURCHES
BIBLICAL PRINCIPLES IN THE EARLY CHURCH

INTRODUCTION

Back when I was young and gung ho as an early candidate for ministry, I was still in a university Arts program. I had sensed a clear call to Christian service. I pestered the dean of theology at my future "seminary" to see if there was some place I could serve as a student pastor. I didn't wait too long. He accepted my request at face value, even though I was many months from graduation with my Arts degree. Within a short time, the director of "home missions" contacted me and asked about my interest in a fledgling congregation that had begun only a week earlier in rented school space. That mission was using the services of a willing retired pastor who was glad for "soon" relief.

That was in February. By April, with denominational sponsorship, the congregation asked me to serve them. I finished my exams for second year Arts, and began my ministry there on Mother's Day of the same year. I was not yet ordained. Moreover, I had more "dare" than "don't you dare," so I set out to organize myself and to some extent, the congregation.

This group was an amalgam of faiths and almost-faithed people who lived in a new community then on the edges of a fresh burgeoning community. Some leaders of the denomination to which I belonged, had surveyed the area and decided to "plant" a church in that neighbourhood. This was post-World War II, when the populace was serious about getting settled into life without the interruptions of war (although the Korean War was now well underway).

Neighbourhoods wanted churches. Churches gave them security. I bought into that scene as if it were gospel. I did not realize yet that the church of our Lord Jesus is an organism, not an organization. I assumed an organizational concept that the church until, by scripture[1] and experience, I realized that both the church and the human body are organisms, organized though they may be.

Someone recently sent me a politically incorrect photograph depicting how things are done in Britain today. It shows 10 men conversing with each other while watching one man do the digging. The 10 are: the human resources manager, the marketing manager, the logistics manager, the technology manager, the project manager, the IT manager, the health and safety inspector, the business manager, the PR manager and the product developer. The man digging is described as the "bloke from Poland."

This is an organization. Translate that to the church as an organization and you simply substitute various church

---

[1] 1 Peter 2:5; Ephesians 2:16; Colossians 3:15; Romans 12:4

officers and the pastor becomes the "bloke from Poland." But an organism involves all 11 of them working together for the building up of the church, not just watching the pastor engaged in digging.[2] An organism does not allow mission to become a spectator sport.

Something in that first congregation didn't quite fit. Maybe it was the concept of organism rather than organization. Perhaps a church started by a group of churches doesn't know its parentage very well. Too many putative fathers, I suspect! Moreover, not all the churches in the larger area were supportive. One pastor, whose member was 10 miles away from him and a half-block from our meeting place, told me not to visit him. He "belonged" downtown, the pastor told me. The member, however, didn't think the other pastor had dibs on him and stayed with us. Other church leaders were supportive. "Any time you find someone from my congregation living in your area, go visit and persuade him to join you," another pastor told me. The latter had a mission mentality.

Something was not quite right about the forming of that church. The rationale for starting it was from a business model "branch plant" mentality. Many years and numerous pastors later, that congregation bred from branch plant chickens has fostered a maintenance mentality. Those birds came home to roost. The church is stalemated. Stale too.

Nonetheless, that congregation blossomed in the mode of Jesus' parable.[3] After three years, I knew that the people needed a full-time pastor, not simply a student serving

---

[2] Ephesians 4:7–16

[3] Matthew 13: 36

11

as a part-time pastor. But it was stony ground and roots were shallow and vulnerable to any exigencies. Nonetheless, I urged the mission board to find such a full-time person and it did. I looked again for another place to add my experience to my zeal. I was "placed" again, this time in a smaller city where another new "cause," as denominational leaders designated such churches, could take root. The soil was better. So was the sower.

This new congregation would have its first worship service two weeks after I moved into the area. The new cause was a baby of the mother church. The mother church was clearly the parent, had bought property and was willing to donate some of its members as missionaries to start the new church. The new cause became a clone of the mother church.

The church began well. After five years, two as a student pastor, and three of them as a full-time pastor, I saw the membership grow to three figures. Moreover, the mother church's finances matched numbers that equaled its givings prior to donating people and scrip to start us up. That church did not think in terms of maintenance; it had a sense of mission. The mother church loaned us its baptistry when we had not yet built one of our own. Today, both mother and clone are prospering.

Decades have passed since those so-called "plantings." My ministry has touched well-established churches too and I have learned much from them. I am no less a follower of Jesus Christ, my Lord and Saviour than when I was gung ho at seminary. In reflection, I wonder what I (we) did right and what I (we) did wrong in forming the new churches.

I have read much literature since then on "church planting" and church growth but I'm not sure even those guru book-writers always have it correct. Generally they persuade us with formulas that if we do this or follow that, some excellent results will appear. Far too often I chafe when I hear the term "church planting" because I've concluded that we don't plant churches; they plant themselves with God's help. Church growth happens if the conditions fit.

What follows in this book is an inspection of my observations on what happened in the New Testament churches. I take heart that they were nearly all dysfunctional. Ephesus was theologically sound but loveless. Corinth's crowd was personality-driven. Even Philippi, the poor but generous church, was personality-conflicted too. What about Laodicea? It didn't even invite the Lord to its meetings! Galatian believers had a serious racial bias. Thessalonian Christians were hung up on dates of the Lord's return. What an ecclesiastical mess! Go through the list and realize the infinite imperfections inherent in the beautiful "Body of Christ." Paul's letters to these churches reflect the abundant aberrations of Christian infancy and instruct us how the great missionary Paul spent so much of his time and energy penning memos or dousing house fires. However, his pen also gave us God's rules to live by in our walk with the Lord Jesus.

Despite the quirkiness of his extended flock, Paul noted some marvelous growth. This is what we hope to learn from within the pages of this document.

PART ONE

Biblical Models

CHAPTER ONE

Start with Conversion

We cannot read about Paul without reading that many of the churches predated him. Starting at Pentecost, great numbers of people, Jews in Jerusalem, Diaspora Jews, God-fearers and interested Greeks staked their claims on the Christian faith. Masses gathered at the steps near the immersion vats leading to the Temple entrance. Peter preached. Three thousand responded positively and were immersed in the vats – not by the Jewish mode of self-immersion – but by the disciples and other converts. Then what?

Many of the 3,000 converts stayed in Jerusalem. Luke describes them as an all-round group. They cared about each other. They journeyed in prayer together. They enjoyed table fellowship in each others' home. Unusual things happened to them and others. They shared their possessions and their lives with each other. They cared about each other. They studied under apostolic leadership. They shared their vibrant faith in Jesus, Messiah and Lord. Luke says it this way:

> They devoted themselves to the apostles' teaching and to the fellowship, to the breaking of bread and to prayer. Everyone was filled with awe, and many wonders and miraculous signs were done by the apostles. All the believers were together and had everything in common. Selling their possessions and goods, they gave to anyone as he had need. Every day they continued to meet together in the temple courts. They broke bread in their homes and ate together with glad and sincere hearts, praising God and enjoying the favour of all the people. And the Lord added to their number daily those who were being saved.[4]

My former professor of philosophy, Dr. F. W. Waters, commented on this passage when he was well aware that his days were numbered. He printed, but never published in 1982, a little booklet of about 200 copies to distribute to a few friends and to his neighbours. Before he died, he told me, he wanted to share something of his faith. This task was in his "bucket list." He personally took the booklets to each resident in his neighbourhood, explaining to those living near him that maybe they knew him from living in their community but they may not have known the values that motivated him. This witness of a 95-year old was titled, *You Can Know God.*[5]

---

[4] Acts 2:42–47

5

Dr. Will Waters survived World War I. He recuperated from his war wounds in a British hospital, and saw the significance of this Acts passage (2:42-47) as a battle cry. "It sounds to me," he wrote, "like the assembling of troops and armament for some great offensive. Even the prayer in which this large company engaged was no 'sweet hour' of rest and peace; it was part of the action, the beginning of the operation – 'and they devoted themselves to it.'" The new church was preparing itself for combat.

And who planted this conflict-ready church? My vote is that it was not planted by humans, and certainly not by aliens or angels. This Jerusalem church was planted by the Spirit of God, using the faith of the people who newly invested their trust in Messiah Jesus as Saviour. They organized for a mission and crusade. Peter and other disciples took part in the formation. They set some leaders aside to share their faith in public. Others were designated to offer acts of service to the needy. The need was mostly among Greek God-fearing widows for whom support was scanty in their social strata.

This group of deacons also preached the gospel. One of that service-oriented group became the protomartyr. The new faith community concurred with such decisions. Stephen died in a hail of rocks thrown by fanatic neocons for his courageous faith declaration.[6] Paul, later the great missionary, stood by, assenting to the assassination, folding his hands over the others' vestments while slobbering gleefully over the despicable deed. Saul/Paul did not know the truth stated decades later by Tertullian: "The blood of the

---

[6] Acts 7:57

17

martyrs is the seed of the church." Pharisee Paul/Saul thought he was winning. Paul didn't plant the Jerusalem church, for sure!

Temple visits became the birthing ground of the new faith community. It was a gathering place anyway, not only for spiritual purposes but also for many business connections. Jerusalem was busier than Rome for commercial purposes. Traders from Asia and Africa brought goods to sell. Merchants from Rome bought shiploads of spices and peppers and figs and clothing material. Money exchanged hands, much of it swapped within the grounds of the Great Temple complex but remote from the sacrificial sites. Since only Jews or other Israelites could enter the confines of the Temple Mount, many Semite traders grew wealthy. The newly formed church thrived.

Jerusalem would need Paul's budding insights soon enough. The fledgling church had trouble in spades, despite the heart-warming Acts 2:42–47 sepia photograph Luke described in his summary of a remarkable day at the south edge of the Great Temple mount. Diseased people challenged the leaders immediately. Could they duplicate the healings done by Jesus?

Sometimes they did succeed in that. A lame beggar, by the power of God, walked when he formerly had sat and asked for alms. The Bible records other victories. Spiritual opponents stirred up trouble as the disciples declared their faith to others. The Jesus folk were imprisoned. Such threats cowed some of the new converts. Rabbinical leaders were split in their opinions of how to deal with threats to their authority and to their faith base. A Jewish leader named

Gamaliel urged restraint. Others pressed for arrests and trials of the convert-heretics.

Not all converts kept faith with their words. Deeds and speech often conflicted, and so a man and wife who promised a faith-donation, kept part of their gift for themselves. Peter exposed their veniality and faced them to the reality that they had lied to God, not just the church. Not much seemed different from the stories of Israelites migrating to Canaan from Egypt! The Jerusalem church birthed at Pentecost had growing pains. But that would not deter its growth, and such agony fostered its resolve.

Hundreds more Pentecost pilgrims departed Jerusalem returning to their communities to carry on with life. They returned to their homes in the Diaspora. What stories they had to tell of their experiences during *Shavuot* that year in Jerusalem!

How did these waves of believers process what they had seen and heard and had come to believe? We can only guess. A good presumption is that they told the account of Jesus, his death and resurrection and the convincing address they heard from one of his followers about how he was the Messiah sent from God to "save" the world. In that way, the three thousand converts of Pentecost multiplied into many more thousands in the centre and fringes of the Roman Empire. And churches formed, not from any one person's planting, but from the Spirit-filled witness of those who heard "the Word" and believed.

Luke specifically points to a conversion of a high-ranking African visitor to *Shavuot* (likely) that year. The account underlines the truth that planting churches was not the priority of the Pentecost people. Luke described this visitor to Jerusalem as an official of an Ethiopian government. He is called a "treasurer," a term later used as pastor or bishop in the New Testament. He may also have been in charge of a harem, since eunuchs found employment in that way.

If he was a proselyte Jew or a god-fearer is also unknown. Nonetheless he was versed in scripture and may have attended the *Shavuot* festivities in Jerusalem without being on the Temple Mount itself. Because he had undergone sexual mutilation, the *Torah* barred him from being on the Temple Mount. "No one who has been emasculated by crushing or cutting may enter the assembly of the LORD."[7]

Obviously the events on Pentecost or *Shavuot* puzzled him. He sought scripture to understand what Peter talked about, namely Jesus, God's anointed one. He was reading Isaiah when the deacon Philip joined him to ask what he was reading and why.

> He was despised and rejected by men, a man of sorrows, and familiar with suffering. Like one from whom men hide their faces he was despised, and we esteemed him not. Surely he took up our infirmities and carried our sorrows, yet we considered him stricken by God, smitten by him, and afflicted. But he was pierced for our transgressions, he was crushed for our iniquities; the punishment that brought us peace was upon him, and by his wounds we are healed . . . It was the LORD's will to crush him and cause him to suffer, and though the LORD makes his life a guilt offering, he will see his

---

7 Deuteronomy 23:1

offspring and prolong his days, and the will of the LORD will prosper in his hand. After the suffering of his soul, he will see the light of life and be satisfied; by his knowledge my righteous servant will justify many, and he will bear their iniquities.[8]

Possibly the Ethiopian's dilemma was compounded by added words from Isaiah: "Let no foreigner who has bound himself to the LORD say, 'The LORD will surely exclude me from his people. And let not any eunuch say, 'I am only a dry tree.'"[9]

Peter's sermon at the southern steps leading to Temple Mount entrances proposed, among other matters, that those far from the restrictions of the *Torah* would find freedom in Jesus. "Repent and be baptized, every one of you, in the name of Jesus Christ for the forgiveness of your sins. And you will receive the gift of the Holy Spirit. The promise is for you and your children and for all who are far off—for all whom the Lord our God will call."[10]

No wonder the court treasurer was bewildered. Was it [11] possible that Jesus was the end result of Isaiah's prophecy? If so, his mutilation would no longer prohibit his full fellowship with God. It seemed to him that God's love is

---

[8] from Isaiah 53

[9] Isaiah 56:3

[10] Acts 2:39, 40

11

inclusive. God welcomed foreigners as his own people, accepted mutilated persons as complete participants in his family and sinful people into his holy fellowship. Philip cleared that for him.

Did the eunuch's mutilation prevent him from using a *mikveh* (ritual immersion vat)? Probably. A leper could not use one unless he was declared healed by a priest. The rite of cleansing a leper is described in Leviticus 14. Once declared clean by a priest, he could participate in all the events of public Hebrew life. However, a eunuch could not change his mutilated condition.

Perhaps the Ethiopian in this Acts passage watched enviously as other *Shavuot* pilgrims immersed themselves and entered freely into the Temple's grand grounds. Thus he raised a question to Philip. "Look, here is water. Why shouldn't I be baptized?"[12] The term "be baptized," suggests that he did not baptize himself. We know little of what followed except that he left that place "rejoicing." Such rejoicing likely led him to share his newfound faith and his acceptance in God's sight with many others. In that way, a community of believers, spurred by the convert and the Holy Spirit, would have formed a church.

Philip was part of a vanguard of an evangelistic thrust into Samaritan territory. That they dared to venture there was a testimony of their convictions. Had not Jesus commissioned his followers to witness in Samaria once they had received the Holy Spirit?[13] Thus Philip preached about

---

[12] Acts 8:37

[13] Acts 1:8

Jesus, baptizing the converts. Samaria was on the "travel alert" of most Jews, so it was not only a stretch of faith for their enterprise but a clear statement that the Good News of Jesus Christ – his life, death, resurrection and teachings – was clearly inclusive for all peoples. Philip's work and results echoed in Jerusalem, where church leaders sent Peter and John to ensure that Philip's success was legitimate. The two leaders verified Philip's work. They then instructed one confused convert, Simon, alias The Great One, that his conversion was incomplete without his receiving the Holy Spirit. Emboldened by Philip's example, John and Peter preached in Samaritan villages as they returned to Jerusalem.

After Stephen's death, possibly two years after Jesus' resurrection, another wave of believers left for their own Diaspora, and while they could be criticized for a lack of faith, their flight to new communities provided impetus for church growth. Wherever they fled they gossiped the gospel. Undoubtedly, as they migrated north and east, sometimes west and south, they met others who had experienced the remarkable *Shavuot* experience on the birthday of the church but now were back home and still puzzled about what had happened to them months before.

A church already existed in Damascus when Saul (a.k.a., Paul) set out to rein in the activities of "The Way," the sobriquet for membership in the new faith. He was hellbent on returning all believers in shackles to face the Sanhedrin court in Jerusalem. What followed may be what psychologists call "formation reaction." It means simply that one becomes zealous against those things that one fears the most.

Psychology may diagnose Saul's response correctly, but the God-factor cannot be explained away. Suddenly, a glorified Jesus confronted Saul on the road to Damascus. Saul was temporary blinded by Jesus' presence in his life. The moment announces Saul's inner awareness of his situation. Saul answered Jesus, "Yes, Lord." In other words, Saul knew full well that his resistance to the gospel resulted from his wrestling with the truth about Jesus as Lord, Son of God, and Messiah, crucified, buried and resurrected. Saul was converted.

That changed not only Saul, but altered the church's missionary understanding of the burgeoning church movement. Jesus always creates a C-change in those he meets. The wise and trusting Ananias welcomed Saul as a brother,[14] inviting a terrified Saul to stay with him. The Holy Spirit descended on Saul. Ananias baptized him. God opened his eyes again and he ate once more to recover strength. Luke records the change:

> Saul spent several days with the disciples in Damascus. At once he began to preach in the synagogues that Jesus is the Son of God. All those who heard him were astonished and asked, "Isn't he the man who raised havoc in Jerusalem among those who call on this name? And hasn't he come here to take them as prisoners to the chief priests?" Yet Saul grew more and more powerful and baffled the Jews living in Damascus by proving that Jesus is the Christ.[15]

---

[14] Acts 9:17

[15] Acts 19b–22

24

Some of the posse accompanying Paul did not like what happened. So when they and other petulants watched him too closely, Saul's new friends helped him escape the city by lowering him over the city wall by night. Saul made his way back to Jerusalem; received encouragement from a Cypriot Levite-Jew named Joseph Barnabas, and slowly won over the cautious converts in Jerusalem's budding church. Paul went off to Arabia for his "seminary" training under God himself. When he returned, he located himself in Antioch near his hometown of Tarsus.

To this point, Luke records no new churches. Some already functioned well. Nowhere (that I can detect) is credit given to someone for planting a church. Moreover, the term "planting a church" does not exist. Early believers did not possess a "branch plant" mentality about growth.

The principle that appears to activate new churches is the conversion of individuals, Jew, Greek, Ethiopian or whatever. This gathering of like-minded individuals, with the infusion of the Holy Spirit, fashions a church. A church forms from the faith held by converts. As Jesus said to his disciples gathered at Banyas in northern Israel, "I give you the keys of the kingdom of heaven [and] I will build my church."[16] Faith is the key that opens us to God. Faith found in his followers allows Jesus to upbuild his church.

---

[16] Matthew 16:17–19

CHAPTER TWO

Intentional Mission

Antioch in Syria became the new centre of gravity for Christians. Begun by Alexander the Great, it next was ruled by Celeucus, one of Alexander's generals. Subsequently five different rulers named Antiochus governed the city, the most notorious of whom was Antiochus Epiphanes. He was *persona non grata* in Jewish circles because of his desecrating their Jerusalem Temple.

Like Delphi, Antioch paid homage to Pythion Apollo. The city also became a magnet for traders and as such was among the most cosmopolitan of cities in the Mediterranean world. Estimate of its peak population suggested a half-million people, more than double the size of Corinth by the time Paul had made Antioch his stepping-out city.

Many Diaspora Jews made Antioch their home. "Jews" became a generic word, for tribal distinctions seemed unimportant to the multi-ethnic city. Paul identified himself as a Jew, not a Benjaminite and Barnabas thought of himself as a Jew[17] even though he was a Levite. Paul addressed people of his faith and ethnicity as "children of Abraham"[18] or "Men of Israel."[19] These were all-inclusive terms but the reality is that "Jew" became the operative designation.

Antioch on the east side of the Orontes River became a remarkably diverse community that accommodated not only Jews but also people of any faith and culture. Visit its riverfront souks on market days, or exchange views in its Roman forum or Greek agora – Antioch had both – and you would meet Antiochenes originating from the far edges of the Mediterranean world. Even the new church in Antioch represented immigrants from Cyrene in North Africa and Niger in Central Africa, the Island of Cyprus and who knows where else! The city was diverse in so many ways – ethnically, socially, religiously, morally, economically and educationally. That made Syrian Antioch ideal for mission-minded believers to make their mark and witness.

The Diaspora of Abraham's children joined themselves to communities not only in Antioch but also throughout the Mediterranean catchment area. Often they lived on the edges of the communities to which they attached themselves to maintain kosher kitchens and habits. They avoided, for the most part, occupations that could make them ritually unclean. They shunned worker groups like guilds that usually embraced a patron deity to be placated when the

---

[17] Galatians 2:15

[18] Acts 13:26

[19] Acts 13:16

28

guilds met. Guild meetings often ended in drunkenness from wine used in deity adulation. Their living on the edges of towns and villages also provided city elders with excuses to cast suspicion on them. Why do they live that way – something to hide, maybe? Are they good subjects of the emperor?

The group of believers in Antioch combined Jews and "God-fearing Gentiles" in their fellowship. Antioch slowly became the leading edge of Christian witness and faith. Yet Jerusalem was not forgotten. Indeed, the believers in Jerusalem, especially the Apostles still stationed there, continued as the reference point for orthodox faith and practice. On the matter of whether Gentile converts needed to become Jews, Peter addressed that Antiochene brothers and sisters with the ultimate solution.

> You know that some time ago God made a choice among you that the Gentiles might hear from my lips the message of the gospel and believe. God, who knows the heart, allowed that he accepted them by giving the Holy Spirit to them, just as he did to us. He made no distinction between us and them, for he purified their hearts by faith. Now then, why do you try to test God by putting on the necks of the disciples a yoke that neither we nor our fathers have been able to bear? No! We believe it is through the grace of our Lord Jesus that we are saved, just as they are![20]

---

[20] Acts 15:7b–11

Before that issue was resolved (although for some detractors it remained unresolved, causing Paul to pen his epistle to the Galatians) the Antioch church resolved to advance a mission. The Bible explains that this action resulted from the direction of the Holy Spirit. "Set apart for me Barnabas and Saul for the work to which I have called them."[21]

That Bible watershed reveals several realities. First, God's Spirit indicated that the two leaders had God's blessing to do the work God intended them to undertake. They were to stop other activities and devote themselves to God's plan for their lives.

Secondly, the itinerary set before them was designed by God's Spirit. This fact reveals that both partners in mission did not select their own objectives.

Thirdly, the church's task of determining God's direction resulted from specific spiritual activities to worship God. In their worship, the church gathered for fasting and prayer, and in that context sensed what God wanted of them.

Fourthly, the task was very specific. The two set out to visit synagogues to tell Jews that Jesus was their Messiah. They then explained that Messiah Jesus was the Son of God, who had lived, died from crucifixion, was resurrected and had ascended into heaven. They did not set out to "plant churches," but to "proclaim the word of God."[22] For that matter, Jesus did not instruct his disciples, "Go into all the world and build branch plants."

---

[21] Acts 13:2b

[22] Acts 13:4

30

Fishing Where the Fish Are

The two "proclaimers" sensed God's leading[23] and travelled to Cyprus, perhaps prompted by the recent report received in Antioch of communities of believers there. Their strategy was consistent for quite a while. They went to synagogues where they were allowed to speak in the gathering and they went primarily to talk to Jews.[24]

The strategy was simple common sense. Jews awaited their Messiah. Paul and Barnabas believed Messiah had come and his name was Jesus. The two had different roles but one purpose. Barnabas, a Levite, appears to have had more "people skills" than Paul. He was called "the son of encouragement."[25] On the other hand, Paul, with less tact, appears both to have taken the leadership and have driven the momentum of the mutual mission.[26] The order is nearly always "Paul and Barnabas."

In their Asian Minor mission, Paul and Barnabas continued with the strategy of teaching in synagogues but they noticed that the power of the gospel message fell on non-Jewish ears. After a period of successes in witnessing and suffering for it at Iconium, Derbe, Lystra and Pisidian

---

[23] Acts 13: 4.

[24] Acts 13: 5.

[25] Acts 4:36; Acts 9: 27; Acts 11: 22, 23; Acts 15: 39

[26] Acts 15:36.

31

Antioch, the two returned to Antioch to report on their work.

In this way, Paul and Barnabas fulfilled an important aspect of their strategy. They were not lone rangers. They were responsible not only to the Lord but to the entire community of believers. In this way, they demonstrated to the entire *ekklesia* (the "called out" company) that witnessing to others must be accompanied by responsibility and accountability to other believers.[27]

The mission moved from Cyprus to mainland Asia Minor (today's Turkey). In their Asian Minor mission, Paul and Barnabas continued with the strategy but they noticed that the power of the gospel message fell on non-Jewish ears. Luke's notes on leadership changed. What began as "Barnabas and Saul" became "Paul and his companions."

Two situations developed here. A third party had joined them, namely John Mark, a relative of Barnabas. But Mark would soon leave the two. Traveler cum church reporter Luke wrote of them as "Paul and his companions."[28] Modesty would deter Luke from telling of his part on the mission. Were other companions accompanying these missionaries too?

Likely Paul was leader of the mission team, which mirrored developments in subsequent missions. Barnabas demonstrated that he was a conciliatory person whereas Paul was an Alpha-type leader who took charge.

The Bible hides no faults. Paul operated on definite principles, although occasionally he offered arcane

---

[27] Acts 14: 26–28.

[28] Acts 13:13

arguments for those values. Peter, on the other hand, sometimes played to the gallery and wanted friends on all sides of Christian theological debates. Paul was not backward in correcting him.[29]

Such personality traits do not necessarily negate the direction of the Holy Spirit. They do, however, tell us that even when God directs his church, the Lord allows room for personality qualities, even quirks, to display themselves. Sometimes our God-given latent gifts happily coincide with the "Gifts of the Spirit."

The mission foray to Cyprus continued to the south coast of Asia Minor. Their foray was remarkably effective. Synagogue members appeared elated at the prospect of Jesus being their Messiah. Were there any in this crowd among those from the *Shavuot* experience in Jerusalem on that great church birthday? It would not surprise me that this group knew the prior experience.

There were detractors of course, some with vicious intent to stone them. Barnabas and Paul elected to move to a different community to share their good news. As in their Cyprus campaign, good and bad things often met in their mission. Some were healed of illness. Some readily received the Gospel. Some threatened the messengers – an organized campaign of a malevolent sort. This pattern repeated itself anywhere Paul and his companions offered their Good News.

When Paul was stoned in Derbe, organized opposition from a great distance arrived to scuttle the team's efforts. Fortunately, Paul recovered well enough to leave Derbe with Barnabas the next morning. They moved on to

---

[29] Galatians 2:11; Acts 11:19–26; Acts 15:2

Lystra, then Iconium and Pisidian Antioch, sites of previous spiritual victories, and returned by ship to the mother city of Syrian Antioch.

Their tasks done, they reported to the Antioch church that previously had consecrated them for service. They gave their accountability. This mission was something of a pilot project, so the mission group thought it important to detail the open doors that led them to see faith among the Gentiles. Just as important, the Jerusalem church, led by James, sent two delegates, Silas and Judas, to Antioch to affirm its blessing on the decision to welcome Gentiles without insisting that they become Jews first.

CHAPTER THREE

Venturing, Learning and Applying

Accountability brought the Antioch *ekklesia* together to wrestle with the issues of gospel and culture. When they decided to affirm non-Jewish believers as co-partners in faith, Paul set out to retrace steps in Asia Minor where Paul and Barnabas had preached the gospel.

This time, the mission team was Paul and Silas – a team affirmed by the Antioch believers. Paul wanted to return to the recent believers and "see how they are doing."[30] Paul also wanted to convey the results of the Antioch and Jerusalem deliberations about Christ and culture. So the strategy changed slightly to become a partly pastoral one. That done, and having gained Timothy as a colleague in the mission, the "team" set out for new territory only to lack the

---

[30] Acts 15:36.

Lord's leading into anticipated mission stations.

Before Paul set out, he and Barnabas had sharp words with each other about this, thus redefining the mission.

> Barnabas wanted to take John, also called Mark, with them, but Paul did not think it wise to take him, because he had deserted them in Pamphylia and had not continued with them in the work. They had such a sharp disagreement that they parted company. Barnabas took Mark and sailed for Cyprus, but Paul chose Silas and left, commended by the brothers to the grace of the Lord.[31]

Whether Paul was correct in his assessment of John Mark we will never know in this life. Barnabas, the "son of encouragement," as he was dubbed, risked inviting and training an immature young man to disciple him in mission work. Cyprus was their beat. It was the Barnabas' home island and he understood the ways and means to work with them. He must have made a difference in Mark's life by staying the course. The evidence is the second Gospel, the Gospel of Mark.

Paul was often argumentative, sometimes insensitive. He was insightful, abrasive, daring (but not ready to adjust to Mark's immaturity), agenda-driven and yet, despite his sharp tongue, and razor judgments, he was a

---

[31] Acts 15:37–40

caring person. He often exhibited a pastoral touch, much of which is evidenced through his several epistles. He saw the value of follow-up. He noted the need of networking with churches new and old. He recognized the urgency of doing the work that he believed God had commissioned him.

This next mission saw Silas as his initial mission companion. Silas is described as a prophet[32] a description perhaps meaning a "declarer of the gospel," a "forthteller," as over against "foreteller." Paul liked what he saw in Silas, and the church endorsed Paul's choice. Their objective: revisit the churches in Asia where the gospel was both declared and received in Paul and Barnabas' initial visit. We must note how ready was Silas to put aside any personal plans in order to help the mission. Another memo: note the daring of Paul to return to the venue of his stoning.

At Lystra, the two plus Luke invited Timothy to join their mission. Believers in the region commended his faith and maturity, speaking well of him to Paul and Silas. Now the mission team was four in number, including Luke. They complemented one another, each with different traits and strengths. Timothy added an ethic mix, since his father was Greek, his mother, Jewish. Timothy's input (Luke's too, for that matter) was especially valuable when Paul irked the Thessalonian Jews and retreated to a safer locale.

The team could report back to Antioch what Luke recorded: "So the churches were strengthened in the faith

_____

[32] Acts 16:32

and grew daily in numbers."[33] Can we deduce from this ministry that mission is not a one-man show? Obviously, Paul saw the value in follow-up ministry. Instruction was crucial. New converts had no "New Testament" yet and Greeks for the most part did not know the Bible that, to date, ended with Malachi.

All went well until Paul's team reached the southern border of Mysia near the Sea of Marmara. At that time the Team stopped dead in its tracks. The wind of the Spirit becalmed them. Luke records: "When they came to the border of Mysia, they tried to enter Bithynia, but the Spirit of Jesus would not allow them to." They had to wait and wait and wait until God sent some signal to move on – some place, any place. The team was "in irons." The Ancient Mariner reflects what the four must have endured:

> Down dropt the breeze, the sails dropt down,
> 'Twas sad as sad could be;
> And we did speak only to break
> The silence of the sea! . . .

> Day after day, day after day,
> We stuck, nor breath nor motion;
> As idle as a painted ship
> Upon a painted ocean.[34]

---

[33] Acts 16:5

[34] Samuel Taylor Coleridge. The Rime of the Ancient Mariner, Part II, lines 106–110; lines 115–119.

Suddenly, there was a breath. God gave Paul and vision to urge him to enter Europe where the person in the dream pleaded for Paul's help. The others on the team took that as God's directive and the team re-embarked for the mission ship, so to speak.

They did sail, from Troas in Asia Minor, to an island that anchored one of the mystery religions, and onto the mainland of Greece itself. The wind filled their spiritual sails and the Spirit breathed new life into the mission.

Mission always stems from God's leading. It is a key principle of church growth. If we learn anything from this stalled episode in Paul's life, we must acknowledge the Apostle's readiness to wait for God's directives, as painful as the delay may have been.

Moreover, his friends on the journey accepted the reality that God had clearly steered Paul to a new mission directive. They readily concurred with this event. Paul would endure much more stalling as his life edged to its conclusion. Mysia was a portent of what would follow.

The Philippian Challenge

The Pauline team stepped from the trading ship that afforded them transport to Neapolis and quickly found the road to Philippi. A century earlier, near Philippi, Octavian, Brutus and Cassius had taken Rome's military Egnatian highway now used by Paul. It ended in victory for Octavian who became Caesar Augustus. The four missionaries sought a different conquest, the battle for the souls of Europe and they wanted to change the battle cry from "Caesar is Lord" to "Jesus is Lord."

Philippi was much different than cities in Asia Minor. It was a Roman colony, populated now with migrating settlers encouraged by Rome, with all the rights and privileges that such a designation awarded it. Very few Jews inhabited the city, the evidence of which is in Paul's failure to find a worshipping community large enough to form a 10-male synagogue. Some scholars disagree with that theory.

Rather, the closest he came to Judaism in Philippi was a gathering of prayer participants along the Gangitis riverbank. These were women, one, a confident single businesswoman named Lydia, is described as "worshipper of God."[35] That was a start.

Lydia was receptive to the influence of the team, since she obviously was on the edge of the Jewish faith, if not yet a proselyte. She responded by opening "her heart to the Lord," and identified herself as a believer. She invited the four members of the Pauline team to sojourn at her villa during their time in the Roman colony. The team put aside its reluctance to wait there, which undoubtedly was based on any possibility of compromise and gossip arising from staying at the home of an unmarried woman. They were safe.

---

[35] Acts 16:14

40

Lydia had no malevolent intentions. She had a number of servants.

Without the Philippians' knowledge of the *Torah*, Paul's group had no reference point with which to connect the city's citizenry to Jesus. A slave girl owned by devotees of Python Apollo, a ventriloquist, was a fortune-teller and shadowed Paul, describing the group as "servants of the Most High God."[36] The detraction gave Paul opportunity to exorcise the girl. At once the change in the young lady became a witness to the power of God and a threat to her owners who earned money from her outbursts.

The result was a posse of angry merchants who insisted to magistrates that the Jews be jailed, stripped and beaten. The accusation by the magistrate that the men were Jews is clear evidence of what today we would call anti-Semitism. Timothy with his Greek background and Luke the reporter assistant escaped the arrest. Like Joseph in Egypt, the end result of his sale to Caravan merchants was positive. "It was to save lives that God sent me ahead of you."[37]

The beating in jail ended as a conversion of the Jailer and his family. The next morning, having recognized his salvation, and fully aware that he could have been punished for beating the Roman citizen Paul, the jailer and his believing household crossed town to the Gangitis River. Together, they were immersed as believers.

---

[36] Acts 16:17

[37] Genesis 45:5

41

A church was born, not planted by Paul or any human missioner, but by the work of God. When Paul and his friends left Philippi, he made the magistrate and others "eat crow" for having ordered a Roman citizen to be flogged. Paul and company must have left there with heads held high and the new faithful in Philippi liberated from any criticism. In fact, the ambience in that city allowed a positive spirit of joy to inhabit the new believers.

Thessalonian Terrorists

One must marvel at how the Holy Spirit used his missioners to establish the faith in Thessalonica, next city on the team's unplanned journey. Luke records that they were in that city for "three Sabbaths.[38] More accurately, Paul and Silas and (perhaps) Luke were in the city for three Sabbaths but were forced to leave to save their lives.

Three weeks is not a long time to establish a church. Bravely, Timothy continued in Thessalonica to instruct new believers and establish them in the faith. Timothy stayed there to firm up the faithful until Paul sent for him to upbuild the new Berean believers when Paul and Silas had retreated from Thessalonica. When disrupters came to Berea, Paul realized he alone was the objective of Jewish vindictiveness. He left for Athens, a city with very few Jews. Timothy and Silas remained in Berea to school the city's new church.

---

[38] Acts 17:2

42

CHAPTER FOUR
God's Athenian Strategy

Caring new believers from Thessalonica and Berea escorted Paul to Athens. The small Jewish population in Athens would not likely organize to hassle Paul. Moreover, the bully crowd that drove Paul and Silas from Thessalonica to Berea consisted largely local rascals whose style and viewpoint would not be welcome in the city of the "divine" Athena, deity of Wisdom.

Lessons learned in Philippi in dealing with non-Jewish people enabled Paul to relate to the Athenians. Enough Jews lived in Athens to form a synagogue, so that gave Paul a tiny toehold. He had come to a city priding itself on culture, debate, education, philosophy – and a pantheon of religious authorities. Most of the spiritual influences were from Greek mythical figures.

The Athenians were well versed in attitudes styled by Stoics, Cynics, Epicureans and Egyptian religions. This was the city of Pericles, Socrates, Plato and Aristotle. The arts flourished. The Parthenon housing Athena's idol was the acme of architectural attraction. "Man," claimed Protagoras, "is the measure of all things." The citizens, or many of them, were erudite people. Religion was often a topic of debate and influenced Athenian behaviours and attitudes.

Enter Paul arriving at Athens' port from Berea via Cape Sounion where respectful sailors deposited Poseidon's idol on the sea floor near his remarkable temple at Sounion. The Berean men took Paul straight to Athens city centre, the agora of Athens. He quickly found a synagogue where he launched a mission to declare Jesus as Messiah, crucified, buried and resurrected. Luke says Paul "reasoned" with synagogue members and God-fearers.

Luke reported that Paul was distressed at the idolatry of the Athenians. In the Panathenian Way, he ventured into a discussion with anyone he met. Idols were abundant and saddened Paul. Little temples dominated the edges of the agora. Pillars upholding buildings were carved with representations of Greek deities.

Few Jews dared to travel the Panathenian Way because of the panorama of images of gods. If they did venture there, the most observant of them would walk with eyes cast downward toward the ground lest their eyes by chance espy an idol – or some other evil. Not so with Paul.

He saw idols for what they were – images made of stone and no more. So he could look at them and not feel that they violated him. His reaction was more of sadness at the vacuity of Greek minds to invest power in created items carved from stone. His workplace was the agora; his audience, strollers on foot to market or business. He challenged them, especially Stoics and Epicureans to consider the possibility of Jesus' death and resurrection. They called him a sparrow, picking up seeds from various religions, hopping here and there formulating his ideas and melding them into his theology.

In turn, they challenged him to offer his ideas to an assembly of the city council. The council, known as the Areopagus, met near the mound of Ares, (Greek) or Mars (Latin). The two names Ares and Mars hint that this was where war councils once met in past days of conflicts with Persia or Sparta. By Paul's time, the setting had become a metro meeting Odeon. Once present, Paul accepted their dare and led, not with scripture that most average Athenians knew nothing about, but with cogent arguments rooted in teachings and ideas from Greek philosophers. In this arena, Paul was in for the fight of his life. He was, however, capable of matching his questioners.

Moreover, he was effective. Some scoffed at Paul's ideas when he spoke of the resurrection. It was not a Greek concept. Moreover, the word for resurrection is *anastasis*. Some listeners understood *anastasia* as a consort of Jesus,

(Jesus and the Resurrection!) like the Egyptian deities Isis and Osiris. Others left the council meeting pondering what it all meant. Some accepted Paul's challenge, the concept of Jesus' death and resurrection, and became followers of the Lord. One convert named Dionysius, by tradition, became a bishop (pastor) of the church in Athens. Again, as in the past, Paul declared the good news of Jesus and the Spirit of God turned the converts into a formidable church.

The Apostle left Athens when he felt his work was done. He headed westward to Corinth, likely by ship and sent messages to Silas and Timothy to join him in Corinth.

CHAPTER FIVE
Growth and Development in Corinth

Paul didn't say why he was leaving Athens. Acts records his departure succinctly. "After this, Paul left Athens and went to Corinth."[39] Thus the reader is given another of Acts' cryptic segues from one story to the next. It doesn't help to speculate whether Paul went to Corinth for predetermined meeting plans with Silas and Timothy or if he felt his brief work in Athens was left in the good care of the Lord's new servants Dionysius, Damaris or others.[40] Paul had trusted God to lead him to Athens. He trusted God's Spirit to cement the new congregation.

Corinth was a well-established city in Paul's time

---

[39] Acts 18: 1.

[40] Smith, T. C. The Broadman Bible Commentary: Acts. p. 105.

and with a long history. It sent émigrés to Italy and Sicily as far back as the eighth century BC.[41] It took second place to Sparta as a result of the Peloponnesian War and was likewise second to Athens in its golden age of the fifth century BC.[42] Both Sparta and Athens lost their powers to Philip of Macedon and the ensuing rule of Alexander. Philip set up a fortress on Corinth's great hill – the Acrocorinth.[43]

Romans destroyed Corinth in 146 BC only to rebuild it in 44 BC under Julius Caesar. Augustus continued the rebuilding after Julius Caesar's death.[44] Roman settlers followed, as did a number of emancipated Greeks from Rome.

The latter group created a resurgence of the Greek language which began to predominate the "official" Latin tongue which Augustus had fostered. In Paul's time Corinth was bilingual although Latin inscriptions became more predominant as the first century AD ended.[45] Meeks notes: "The government was typical of a Roman colony, with annually elected *duoviri* and *aediles*. The depth of this Romanization, however, should not be exaggerated." That is,

---

[41] Papahatzis, Nicos. Ancient Corinth. p. 18.

[42] Papahatzis, Nicos. op. cit. p. 19.

[43] Papahatzis, Nicos. op. cit. p. 20.

[44] Ibid.

[45] Ibid.

48

Greek was still a factor even though Latin inscriptions predominated.[46]

Corinth was located inland, not quite equidistant from its two ports, Lechaion to the north on the Gulf of Corinth and Cenchraea to the southeast on the Saronic Gulf (also known as the Bath of Helen). Walls from Corinth protected Lechaion stretching from the port right into the heart of ancient Corinth.

Three significant communities coexisted alongside Corinth, the ports of Lechaion and Cenchraea and the sacred city of Isthmia which hosted the Panhellenic Isthmian Games every two years.[47] The Sanctuary of Poseidon dominated the village at Isthmia. Lechaion (var. Lechaeum) and Cenchraea held importance because the ports provided relatively safe harbours, whereas seafarers disliked rounding the weather-bound tip of the Peloponnesus, especially in winter. Barclay writes:

> Of all the strategic centres Corinth was the most commanding . . . Men called it "the city of two Seas." They spoke of it as "the bridge of Greece," for every single item of traffic and of commerce that did not travel by sea had to pass through Corinth on its journey from north to south.

Not only did north and South traffic pass through it;

---

[46] Meeks, Wayne A. The First Urban Christians. p. 47.

[47] Papahatziz, Nicos. op. cit. p. 30.

east and west traffic had to take the same route. The extreme southern point of Greece is called Cape Malea and, in ancient days, to sail round Cape Malea was the equivalent of sailing around Cape Horn in the days of sail. It was a journey so dangerous that there were two famous Greek proverbs, "Let him who thinks of sailing round Malea forget his home," and "Let him who sails around Malea make his will" . . . The ships from all the world found their way into the quays of Corinth, where the triremes, the famous ships of Greece, had first been built.[48]

Both ports were centres of transhipping. Goods were unloaded at either port and transhipped across to the other port via the *diolkos*. The *diolkos* (from *dielko*, "to haul")[49] was a paved roadway with wooden rollers employed to drag smaller ships across the isthmus to the opposite gulf. More probably, the *diolkos* enabled large wagons on wheels to carry smaller vessels along its route.[50] Toward the end of Paul's life, Nero actually tried to build a canal from one gulf to the other using workmen and slaves. But the attempt lasted only three months and failed.[51] During Paul's ministry he would have seen the ships being transported along the *diolkos*. He also used the port of Cenchraea (var. Cenchreai,

---

[48] Barclay, William. <u>Ambassador for Christ</u>. pp. 111-112.

[49] Papahatzis, Nicos. <u>op. cit</u>. p. 28.

[50] <u>ibid</u>.

[51] Papahatzis, Nicos. <u>op. cit</u>. p. 29.

Cenchreae) himself, probably arriving in Corinth and certainly in leaving it.[52]

Corinth was a cosmopolitan city of considerable wealth. With its affluence were attached many aspects both positive and negative. It was a multilingual, ethnically diverse, erudite city – and because of its port activities – world-conscious and international. The flourishes on the capitals of its building pillars appeared distinct from the plainer capitals of either the earlier Doric or Ionic traditions. In a way, the embellishments of Corinthian capitals reflected the flourishing Corinthian style of living.

It was also a city of lewd activity. Its very name "Corinth" lent itself to a reputation of drunkenness and immorality. William Barclay describes the situation into which Paul entered to share his witness of his Lord.

> Corinth "was one of the [wickedest] cities in the world. There was actually a Greek word 'to play the Corinthian' which meant to live in drunken and immoral debauchery" . . . On the Acropolis there was the Temple of Aphrodite . . . the shrine of the Greek goddess of love. Her temple had a thousand priestesses who were sacred prostitutes and for the profit of the goddess they descended to the streets each evening to ply their immoral trade. It had become a Greek proverb, 'Not every man can afford a journey to Corinth.' It was not only the open vices which flourished in Corinth but the foreign sailors

---

[52] Acts 18:18.

and traders coming from the ends of the earth brought in with them strange and recondite vices until Corinth became at one and the same a synonym for luxury and for filth."[53]

An Initiation of Christian Witness

The Bible does not say specifically who started the church in Corinth. Certainly it was not Paul. He may have received reports of a church already in existence there and left Athens to see for himself. Aquila and Priscilla may have been the initiators of the church because they preceded Paul. Perhaps the believers were those who heard the gospel message from travellers from the north – Berea (var. Beroea), Thessalonica or Philippi.

More likely, the witnesses came from travellers stopping by Corinth on their way east or west by ship. Possibly, perhaps probably, the *Shavuot* pilgrims spread the word even before Aquila, Priscilla and Paul found Corinth. In any event, the Lord has always gone ahead of anyone intent on obeying him. At the empty tomb an angel told Jesus' disciples, "Go and tell my brothers to go to Galilee; there they will see me."[54] Jesus was there before his disciples arrived.

We know that Paul was in Corinth during the

---

[53] Barclay, William. op. cit.. pp. 113, 114.

[54] Matthew 28:10

governance of the proconsul Gallio. He likely was appointed to his post in July, AD 51.[55] We also know that Aquila and Priscilla were expelled from Rome under an edict from the emperor Claudius. Claudius created a Diaspora for Jews because of the preaching of one Chrestus (does that mean Christ?). F. F. Bruce suggests a more precise dating for Paul's presence in Corinth: "When he [Paul] had completed 18 months in Corinth (say, from the autumn AD 50 to the spring of 52), he left that city and crossed the Aegean to Asia.[56]

Scholars suggest this Chrestus could have been another name for preaching about Christ.[57] This expulsion from Rome brought the couple to Corinth. If Aquila and Priscilla were not the initiators of Christian faith in Corinth – and perhaps they were – they certainly were mature examples of Christian faith who gave stability to the disparate group of Corinthian believers.

F. F. Bruce suggests the possibility that Priscilla may have been a gentile and from an established Roman family and that

> Priscilla may not have come personally within the scope of the expulsion edict – she may not have been

---

[55] Smith, T. C. op cit. p. 107.

[56] Bruce, F. F., The Pauline Circle, p. 52.

[57] Smith, T. C., op. cit. p. 101.

Jewish by birth – but she went into exile with her husband . . . They have been envisaged as the kind of business people who had [leatherwork shops] branches in several cities.[58]

Networking

Paul's initial contacts in Corinth were Aquila and Priscilla. The writer of Acts indicates they were tentmakers (leather workers). In some texts (the Bezan Text and an old Latin Version)[59] the comment on their occupation is missing. So many other texts support his tentmaking experience that Paul's tentmaking background is little in doubt.

Paul said only that he worked with his own hands (1 Cor. 4:12 *ergazesthai tais idias chersin*), presumably, though not necessarily at a trade. Luke . . . Assumed this and even identified Paul as a tentmaker (Acts 18:3: *skenopois*). Luke was dependent here on tradition, a tradition, moreover whose historical reliability is not in doubt. One textual problem can be resolved easily but needs at least to be mentioned. In a few Western manuscripts (D d gig) the entire clause 'For they were tentmakers by trade' is missing, due probably to an oversight . . .

Some say that Paul learned his trade from his father,

[58] Bruce, F. F. op. cit., p. 47.

[59] Ramsay, William M. St. Paul the Traveller and Roman Citizen, p. 253.

adding that his father thereby conformed to the rabbinic maxim 'Whoever does not teach his son a craft teaches him to be a robber . . . ' At the age of thirteen, give or take a year or so, Paul would have begun his apprenticeship and would have spent his days, except for Sabbaths and holidays, in his fathers' workshop (a shop, incidentally, that may have been responsible for his family's acquisition of Roman citizenship if, as has been suggested, the tents there had proved useful in a Roman military campaign) . . . Paul's apprenticeship may have lasted two – perhaps three – years, in an atmosphere of strict discipline and demanding standards, so that when he finished his training he was as skilled in leather working as his father, with skills that would have been widely recognized and admired . . .

At the conclusion of his apprenticeship Paul might have been given his own set of tools. The requisite knives and awls, incidentally, would have made tentmaking as easily portable trade, a fact that helps Paul's eventual use of his trade as his means of support during his travels as a missionary . . .

One could stay up to a week without taking advantage of one's host, though three days were deemed most appropriate, a convention scrupulously followed by Paul, at least according to Acts . . .

This arrangement distinguished Paul from the poorest artisans and unskilled workers of a city; they frequently had to live in the backs of their shops or even in the streets. It also distinguished him from those travelling Cynics who chose . . . to live in public buildings and to support themselves by begging.

Paul's practice of living in Christian households should also be distinguished from the institution of hospitality. That was . . . short term, a week at the most, and Paul was no permanent guest, even though, as an apostle of Christ, he could have imposed himself on a host for extended periods of time (see 1 Thess. 2:7; *en barei einai*; cf. 1 Cor. 9:5– 15.) [60]

From Corinth, Paul wrote to the believers in Thessalonica who were not working, due to their expectation of the imminent parousia. Why work if Jesus is returning soon? His letter offered the example of his own employment and that he continued to work and work hard.

Paul's own statement that he "worked night and day" (1 Thess. 2:9) [reminds] us how much of Paul's time was spent at his trade . . .
This expression suggests that Paul began working before sunrise and continued through much of the day . . .
To judge from apprentices' contracts and from scattered sources elsewhere, the usual workday consisted of daylight hours only, that is "from sunrise to sunset," as the expression went. Paul's working before sunrise, therefore, was unusual . . .

---

[60] Hock, Ronald F. The Social Context of Paul's Ministry, pp. 20– 32.

Far from being at the periphery of his life, Paul's tentmaking was actually central to it."[61]

Networking with Aquila and Priscilla gave Paul considerably more scope in his witness and offered him additional credibility, e.g., his appeal to Thessalonica as a "working" person. It introduced him to the travellers who came to the Panhellenic Games and required someone of his craft. It introduced him to sailors who needed work for their ships and it provided him with income so that he was not seen to be a leech living on the avail of others. He showed that everyone could witness to Christ in their employment opportunities. Tentmaking greatly enlarged Paul's sphere of influence.

Corinth's Church Composition

The Corinthian church was a mixture of many backgrounds. It comprised Jews and Greeks – and likely persons from various ethnic backgrounds, just as in Antioch.[62] Similarly, Corinth seems to have embraced believers from every economic background. Wayne A. Meeks makes a case for the place of the wealthy among those in the Corinthian fellowship.

Many slaves and freedmen travelled as agents of

---

[61] Hock, Ronald F. op. cit. p. 67.

[62] Acts 13:1.

their masters or mistresses, like members of Chloe's household who told Paul in Ephesus about Corinth's troubles (1 Cor. 1:11).

> Gaius (1 Cor. 1:14; Rom. 16:23) has a good Roman praenomen, thus resembling several Corinthians Christians already mentioned, but in addition he has a house ample enough to accommodate all the Christian groups in Corinth meeting together (Rom. 16:23).
> He is evidently a man of some wealth. The same is true of Crispus, whose office as *archisynagōgos* shows he not only has high esteem in the Jewish community but is also probably well to do.
> It is noteworthy that these two are singled out by Paul as people whom he personally baptized at the beginning of Christianity in Corinth (1 Cor. 1:14). It is tempting to assume that the third person mentioned in the same context, Stephanos, the members of whose household were the very first converts (*aparchē*) in Achaia (1 Cor. 15:15), was also a person of wealth. That would be too hasty an inference, however.

> Erastus is named with an official title related to his role in the city: "*oikonomos tēs poleōs*," which could mean either a public official charged with administering public funds or property perhaps an aedile, or someone who was a public slave.[63]

At the same time, many seemed to have had little by

---

[63] Meeks, Wayne A. op. cit. p. 57.

way of status or wealth and could be listed on a lower socioeconomic scale. As John Gager points out, in Paul's first letter to Corinth, he inadvertently provided a glimpse at the social constituency of earliest Christianity:

> 'Not many of you were wise according to worldly standards,' he says, 'not many were powerful, not many were of noble birth; but God chose what is foolish in the world . . . what is weak in the world . . . what is low and despised in the world.')1 Corinthians 1:26–28).[64]

Corinth was also made up of those who were converted from various states of ungodliness. Such is the nature of conversion that God accepts all those who claim his salvation and honour Jesus' lordship. Indeed, the Corinthians needed a reminder of their backgrounds and Paul provided it for them.

> Do not be deceived: neither the sexually immoral nor idolaters nor adulterers nor male prostitutes nor homosexual offenders nor thieves nor the greedy nor drunkards, nor slanderers, nor swindlers will inherit the kingdom of God. And that is what some of you were. But you were washed, you were sanctified you were justified in the name of the Lord Jesus Christ and by the Spirit of our God.[65]

---

[64] Gager, John G. Kingdom and Community: The Social World of Early Christianity, p. 94.

[65] 1 Corinthians 6:9–11.

Providing Spiritual Life in Corinth

Several individuals can be named as contributing significantly to the establishing of a mature church in Corinth. The names that follow had a significant part in "making the faith work" in Corinth.

Aquila and Priscilla

The couple known as Aquila and Priscilla was obviously capable of forming the faith foundations for those in the spiritually and morally unstable climate of Corinth. This couple had known expulsion and so were acquainted with the possibilities of persecution for their convictions. They also had a stabilizing effect of immature believers.

We see an example of this required maturity as the couple moved to Ephesus. There they encountered a charismatic speaker name Apollos from Alexandria. He was not charismatic in the Holy Spirit sense of the word, however, because he knew nothing of the Holy Spirit. Priscilla and Aquila introduced Apollos to God on a different level, namely the level of conversion, not just repentance. His speaking had been on the order of John the Baptist, inviting, urging people to confess their sins before God. He baptized those who repented. But Aquila and Priscilla insisted that his baptism was invalid because it did not come from a complete conversion. Thus he was baptized as a believer in Jesus as Saviour, Lord and Messiah and he received the Holy Spirit.

The implications continue to this day. When is baptism real? It must involve conversion – an idea which challenges any "baptism" by whatever name if it is without the presence of the Holy Spirit. He convicts us not only of sin but of salvation in Jesus Christ.

Paul

Paul obviously was a major faith "founder" in Corinth. A better word to describe Paul's participation in Corinth is "establisher." He helped set the church in a firmer foundation than before he visited. Visit is the operative word but it was an extended visit. The church existed before he arrived. He began to network not only with those in his craft but with those in his faith foundation, that is, the Jews. Paul used the synagogue as his launching pad and continued as was his style elsewhere, to explain the messianic hope found in Jesus, and of the cross which provided the sacrificial atonement[66] for all sins and of the resurrection[67] which was evidenced in them by God's gift of the Holy Spirit.[68]

---

[66] 1 Corinthians 5:7.

[67] 1 Corinthians 15:22.

[68] 1 Corinthians 15:45.

Paul's continuing presence in the Corinthian church whether by correspondence, in person or by vicarious Christian leaders, meant that the church grew in the face of social, cultural, economic and personality challenges. The fact that he remained in Corinth for an extended period – 18 months, instead of his Thessalonian sojourn of three Sabbaths[69] – suggests his concern that Corinth required longer-term leadership.

New Christians do not mature overnight and few in Corinth seemed to understand the extent of maturation they needed. Paul understood, as this book will note in the presentation of challenges with which Paul had to deal.

Apollos

Some time after Paul had left, Apollos arrived in Corinth. Very quickly, Apollos gathered a coterie of admirers and exercised some considerable influence over them.[70] Obviously he was respected for his eloquence, maybe more than was Paul.[71]

Whether Apollos was responsible for the clique that developed under his aegis is not clear. We only know that Corinth experienced an "Apollos faction" and that Paul

---

[69] Acts 17:2.

[70] 1 Corinthians 3:4.

[71] 2 Corinthians 10:10; 11:6.

needed to confront the Corinthians with this failing. Whatever influence Apollos had in Corinth, it did affect the life of the maturing body of believers.

Lay Leaders

Corinth experienced a number of missionary and lay leaders who both contributed to or detracted from the spiritual health of the developing congregation. Silas and Timothy were two of these. Their arrival from Macedonia permitted Paul to spend more time in evangelism, especially among Corinth's gentiles. Titius Justus, "a worshipper of God," and the once-president of the synagogue, Crispus and family, gave witness to their faith and were baptized.[72] Sosthenes, a subsequent synagogue "ruler" created controversy and difficulty for Paul and other Christians but his negativity eventually realized a boon for the church.[73] This leadership derived from Paul's early missionary experience. Wayne Meeks notes that

> from the beginning the Pauline mission was a collective enterprise, with something that can loosely be called a staff. Its corporate nature was one of the most effective elements in the mission's successful adaptation to what Gerd Theissen calls

---

[72] Acts 18:7, 8.

[73] Acts 18:12–17.

"socioeconomic factors" of its urban territory. This arrangement for planting, nurturing, and connecting the Christian household cells was probably not Paul's invention but something he learned at Antioch. Indeed, Ollrog argues shrewdly that Paul's missionary career began as a 'fellow worker' of Barnabas. When Barnabas and Paul split, after the confrontation described in Gal. 2:11–14, each took one or more partners. In the New Testament reports, none of the other apostles, such as Peter, Apollos, or Philip, seems to have done that.[74]

Legal Status: Gallio

Unwittingly, the proconsul Gallio made a major contribution to the Corinthian Christians. By his court judgment, he affected Christian proclamation elsewhere. Jews came to Gallio arguing that Paul had blasphemed by trying to persuade Jews to worship God in disobeying the law. Judaism was legal, of course. But Gallio made an imperial policy toward the Christians. "To be a judge of such matters," he said, "I have no mind."[75] He did not want to deal with "words" and "names," he said, but only with "deeds." Since "deeds" were not involved in this dispute, Gallio dismissed all charges against Paul.[76] Paul's preaching

---

[74] Meeks, Wayne A. op. cit. p. 133.

[75] Acts 18:15.

[76] Ibid.

activity had now been judged to be legal by Rome!

Ten Challenges in Corinth

Since the Corinthian church comprised both Jews and Gentiles, the background of each provided significant behavioural differences. Jews had the law, which as Paul explained to the Galatians, the law was a school teacher.[77] Jews, therefore already enjoyed a code of moral conduct and system of values which were comparable to the teaching and preaching of Paul or the other leaders.

Pagans, on the other hand drew their ethics and morality from a variety of teachers and philosophies, many of which flew in the face of Christian virtues. Sorting this out became a challenge and a series of challenges to the infant *ekklesia* (church) in Corinth. Epicureans, for example, held no view of the afterlife and therefore lived existentially for the moment.

Yet, some aspects of Epicureanism lent themselves to Christian comparisons, such as a sense of unity and a lack of factionalism.[78] Some Stoics were much interested in the cosmos and held to monotheism – and that matched Paul's emphasis on unity.[79]   No doubt, Paul played on the

---

[77] Galatians 3:24.

[78] Meeks, A. Wayne. op. cit., p. 84.

[79] Meeks, A. Wayne. op cit. p. 91.

similarities as he did in Athens[80] in order to attract such philosophers and sometimes to distinguish Jesus' Way from the others. Individual Stoics, Epicureans or Cynics may not have been part of the Corinthian church but the ambiences of their ideas were always adjacent in ancient Achaea.

Consider some 10 of among scores of challenges which Paul, in particular, had to address mostly through his correspondence with the Corinthians. These are not necessarily presented in either chronological occurrence or in priority of importance.

1. Challenge: Cultural Crossovers

Paul and the others faced a formidable task in cross-culturalism. When Jews and non-Jews met in a Christian context, they had to wrestle with both Jewish and pagan traditions. Is there a middle ground for community? The Jewish tradition involved the concept of *halakah*, the "way one walks with God." The pagan Greek society was involved in obliging many deities and patron gods.

One way in which Paul tried to develop this commonality was in the gift collected for the poor in Jerusalem. The purpose of the gift was "to alleviate the needs of the poor."[81]

---

[80] Acts 17:28.

[81] Banks, Robert. Paul's Idea of Community. p. 168.

Another way in which he managed to raise the level of Christianity in Corinth and elsewhere was to elevate the value of women.[82] True, an adverse comment about women appears in his charge to Corinth but surely that was a very specific issue of which a scholar can only surmise.[83] He certainly gave praise and privilege to Phoebe[84] in Cenchraea and both encouragement and trust to Priscilla in Corinth.[85]

Perhaps it was Paul's style and method to divert attention from the minutiae of Jewish and pagan tracts to something of higher mutual interest. Yet Paul had also to warn the Jews about their failure to accept Messiah, and the pagans for a continuance in pagan life styles, i.e., in buying meat which had been butchered (as a dedicated offering to idols)[86] and orgy behaviour at the remembrance of the Lord's Supper.[87]

2. Challenge: Personal Purity

Paul's Jewish sense of *halakah*, of walking with

---

[82] Banks, Robert. op. cit. p. 158.

[83] 1 Corinthians 14:34.

[84] Romans 16:1

[85] 1 Corinthians 16:19; Acts 18:2.

[86] 1 Corinthians 8:1 ff.

[87] 1 Corinthians 11: 27–34.

God, was an issue already understood by the Jews in the Corinth believer group. Paul needed to address the pagan aspects of purity with the new pagan converts to Christ. Some had come to the Lord out of a society in which paedophilia or temple prostitution was commonplace.

Hence he wrote that, "Dear friends, let us purify ourselves from everything that contaminates body and spirit, perfecting holiness out of reverence for God."[88] The strain of right living permeates the two letters to the Corinthians, demonstrating that the need to challenge impurity must have been a constant struggle.

3. Challenge: Recognizing Divine Gifts

The theme of recognizing divine gifts recurred not only in the Corinthian[89] but in the Roman[90] and Ephesian'[91] catchment areas as well. Paul noted that pride tended to accompany the spiritual gifts (graces, charisms) which God had provided for the edification of his church in Corinth.[92] Gifts, Paul reminded the Corinthians, are the Spirit's to offer

---

[88] 2 Corinthians 7:1.

[89] 1 Corinthians 12:1 ff.

[90] Romans 12: 1 ff., esp. 12:3–8.

[91] Ephesians 4:7–13.

[92] 1 Corinthians 12:12–26.

68

and determine for the benefit of the entire church and for the work of the gospel.[93] Apparently, the Corinthians looked upon these "graces" as status symbols and judged one another by the gift and the task each was given to accomplish.

4. Challenge: Resurrection Hopefulness

Fundamental to Paul's belief system was the concept of bodily resurrection.[94] This was basic to his preaching and teaching. In Corinth some disputes arose among the church family about the resurrection. Their convoluted ideas about resurrection ranged from what happened to people who died before Jesus returns and what happens to the living when he does return.[95]

Moreover, in the mix of non-Pharisaic Jews and varied Greek opinions of life after death, some proposed that resurrection could not happen at all. Paul states emphatically that resurrection is a basic part of the salvation experience.[96] Resurrection is much more than a promise to Paul. It is a reality because God has sealed our resurrection by giving us the Holy Spirit as a form of resurrection's "down

---

[93] 1 Corinthians 12:7.

[94] 1 Corinthians 15:3–8.

[95] 1 Corinthians 15:35 ff.

[96] 1 Corinthians 15:2.

payment."[97]

Yet the acceptance and implication of this crucial teaching needed Paul's full endorsement. Paul comes close to belabouring the importance of the resurrection he so readily accepted as fact for himself. Meeks stresses this reality. "We see . . . that the implications of belief were not automatic. The spelling out of the meaning of even so central a belief as the resurrection was a dialectical process. What we call crudely, its social consequences were an integral part of that process."[98]

5. Challenge: Victory Through Adversity

Some of the "success" fertility theologies of pagan cults, such as Aphrodite, may have influenced Christians in Corinth to think that faith in Christ meant continuous success and happiness. Paul needed to address the concept that faith in Christ has no guarantee of success in this life.

Paul therefore spent part of his second recorded letter in spelling out the expectation of suffering and decline. He offered himself as an example, "We are hard pressed on every side, but not crushed; perplexed, but not in despair; persecuted, but not abandoned; struck down, but not

---

[97] 2 Corinthians 5:5.

[98] Weeks, Wayne A. op. cit. p. 183.

destroyed."[99] To Paul, suffering gave him fellowship with Christ and though he did not court it, he realized the privilege of suffering just as Jesus had suffered for him and all believers.[100]

6. Challenge: Living Like Christ

Paul needed to emphasize the reality of the new birth which comes from Christ. "No matter how many promises God has made, they are 'Yes!' in Christ."[101] He told the Corinthians that they were not retrofits of human beings but that Christ had made them entirely new creatures. "If anyone is in Christ, he is a new creation; the old has gone, the new has come!"[102] The concept of being *in* Christ allows us to live *like* Christ. Commented William Barclay, "Over and over again Paul used a little phrase to tell people what he meant. That phrase was *in Christ*. He felt that his life and he himself were in Christ. Sometimes he put it the other way around and said that Christ was in him."[103]

Greeks used two words for our English word "*new.*"

---

[99] 2 Corinthians 4:8, 9.

[100] 1 Corinthians 1:9; 2 Corinthians 6:2–10; Philippians 3:10; Gager, John G., op cit., p. 8.

[101] 2 Corinthians 1:20.

[102] 2 Corinthians 5:17.

[103] Barclay, William. op. cit., p. 176.

One uses "*neo*" as a prefix meaning "new." "*Neo*" means "*new in time*," but it carries with it no connotation of being "*new in quality*." Paul did not use "*neo*" when he wrote to the Corinthians about "*new creation*" or "*new creature*." Paul used a different word — *kaine* — meaning "*new in kind*, of a *different order*."[104] He meant that when the Corinthians accepted Christ as Saviour, they moved from chronological and temporal time into eternal existence. They were born into eternal life.[105]

7. Challenge: God-given Self-worth

Paul needed to let the Corinthians discover the dignity which God gives to every one of his children. "From now on we regard no one from a worldly point of view," Paul told the Corinthians.[106] The Apostle also wanted the Corinthians to see themselves in God's light.

Paul addressed this issue, recognizing that when humans see themselves as God sees them, worthy of Christ's death on the cross to save them, that motivation may elevate their view of themselves. He used the metaphor of the Temple, much as Peter did in addressing his flock in western

---

[104] Fisher, Fred. 1 & 2 Corinthians, p. 343.

[105] Beasley-Murray, G. R. The Broadman Bible Commentary: 2 Corinthians. p. 42.

[106] 2 Corinthians 5:16.

72

Asia Minor as "living stones."[107] "Do you not know that your body is a temple of the Holy Spirit, who is in you, whom you have received from God? You are not your own; you were bought with a price. Therefore, honour God with your body."[108] In this instance, however, Paul also draws upon the concept that Christ has ransomed us because he loves us.[109]

8. Challenge: Giving as Grace

Paul began to realize that his converts in Corinth had failed the test of true giving. God's love is in giving and God graces his followers with the joy of generosity.[110] Paul challenged his flock in Corinth to keep their promise and send their relief package to the believers in Jerusalem. Giving expanded their horizons and sent a signal of an inner grace. "God lives a cheerful (*hilaron*) giver," wrote Paul to Corinth.[111] In using the adjective *hilaron* Paul suggested the exhilaration that generosity provides to the donor.

Paul hints here that the last part of a person to be

---

[107] 1 Peter 2:5.

[108] 1 Corinthians 7:19.

[109] Mark 10:45; 1 Timothy 2:6.

[110] Matthew 6:21–23; 2 Corinthians 9:1–15.

[111] 2 Corinthians 9:7.

baptized is his wallet or her purse. He pointed the Corinthians to the ultimate example of giving in Jesus. "Thanks be to God for his indescribable gift!"[112]

9. Challenge: Unity in Diversity

As Robert Banks points out, the world in which Paul ministered was a world with clashing viewpoints and therefore clashing communities. Roman ideas slowly were replacing Greek ones just as Latin slowly was replacing the Greek language. Corinth was no exception. Within the city of Corinth the church was likewise in a state of flux. Banks points out that Paul was capable of "rolling with the punches," and took transition as a fact of life.

> It was through interaction with the society about him, as well as involvement with his communities, that Paul came to hold the views expressed in his letters, not through theological contemplation removed from the cut and thrust of daily life . . .
> He was . . . under pressure to deepen his convictions in order to deal with new difficulties that had appeared. Paul's understanding of community is never static or frozen into a theological system. It is a living thing, always open to development and in touch with the practicalities of the moment.[113]

---

[112] 2 Corinthians 9:15.

[113] Banks, Robert. op cit. p. 6.

Corinthian Christians were somewhat factious. Paul heard via the Christian grapevine[114] that the fellowship had developed cliques, each of which treated their leaders like religious "superstars." The division was evident in four parties, one devoted to Peter, one to Apollos, one to Paul and one to Christ.[115] Paul answers the problem by asking if Christ is divided.[116] Barclay offered that "by far the greatest leap of originality that Paul made was his conception of all men being one in Christ Jesus."[117]

The obvious answer is "no!" Paul continues to explain that to transfer adoration to individual leaders is to miss the point of the gospel. Christians are a new community, created not for division but for unity and to glorify God.[118]

10. Challenge: Accepting Authority

Christian freedom and accountability became issues in the early Corinthian church. Freedom issues centred

---

[114] 1 Corinthians 1:11.

[115] 1 Corinthians 1:12.

[116] 1 Corinthians 1:13.

[117] Barclay, William. op. cit., p. 178.

[118] 1 Corinthians 1:31.

around sexual behaviour,[119] civil legal actions,[120] marriage responsibilities,[121] and food offered to idols.[122] In some instances Paul's answer is one he knows is from the Lord[123] while in other situations he hedges[124] and at times he offers his reader a situation ethic, such as that of eating food which had been dedicated to a pagan deity.[125]

Paul found it necessary to insert himself and his teaching into the Corinthian situation on some issues. He vindicated his apostleship by reminding the Corinthians that he was commissioned by the Lord himself.[126] He used that authority in dealing with many of the issues which arose from the immaturity of the early church. Paul knew he must exert his authority reasonably and not from a dictatorial perspective, so he argued his case carefully to justify his authoritative comments.[127]

---

[119] 1 Corinthians 5:1.

[120] 1 Corinthians 6:1 ff.

[121] 1 Corinthians 7:1 ff.

[122] 1 Corinthians 8:1 ff

[123] 1 Corinthians 7:10.

[124] 1 Corinthians 7:6, 7, 40.

[125] 1 Corinthians 8:9.

[126] 1 Corinthians 4:9; 1 Corinthians 9:1, 2; 1 Corinthians 12:28.

[127] 1 Corinthians 9:15.

Summary

The church in Corinth developed from infancy with a divergence of ethnic and spiritual partners to become a living, active "body of Christ."[128] It endured great growing pains, distractions from quarrelsome Jews and from disparate backgrounds among its Gentile partners. The leadership was varied and mature, at least from people like Aquila and Priscilla, Silas and Timothy, Paul and Phoebe – if Phoebe can be included as a partner in the Corinthian fellowship.

Credit to the success of the Corinthian church must be given, in part, to a nonbeliever, the Roman proconsul Gallio. His legal decision helped Paul and the other gospel proclaimers to surmount some of the Jewish invective. God was at work in Caesar's deputy! The church then was free to preach, teach and grow on its own terms. Paul was also able,

---

[128] 1 Corinthians 12:13.

because of his relatively long stay in Corinth, to instruct, by letter, the church at Thessalonica.

Paul, however, was a principal instrument of establishing the Corinthian church. He helped them grow better roots. His familiarity with the situation, his connection to the converts, his on-the-spot availability and his obvious love and concern for the church led him back to minister by weighty correspondence and several emissaries. Moreover, the impact of his correspondence continues as a guide and grace for all Christians until Christ returns.

CHAPTER SIX
Ephesus

Paul left Corinth sailing via Cenchrea, heading ultimately for a rendezvous (likely) with the Jerusalem church. He visited a synagogue in Ephesus, met the leaders, who, in turn, asked him to tarry and exegete the scriptures to them. He said he would return, "I will come back if it is the Lord's will."[129] Paul quickly found passage to Caesarea and touched base with the home church, kept his vow and headed once more to Antioch.

No doubt Paul huddled with the leaders in Antioch to share what had happened both from them and to them. He had much to report. The Lord was using the declaration of Jesus' Good News to lead converts into discipleship. The Lord was establishing churches throughout the

---

[129] Acts 18:21

79

Mediterranean region. Each was a church comprising Jews and Gentiles. Undoubtedly Paul related to the Antiochenes the various forms of opposition he encountered. He had many more positive rejoicings to share than the negatives.

Then, he travelled once more, by road, retracing former pathways past the other Antioch, Derbe, Lystra and other Galatian or Phrygian communities. He had much remedial work to do there, considerable correcting and proffered much encouragement to conflicted new Christians.

Subsequently, he moved back to Ephesus. Paul settled in for a long stay. His first item of business was to correct false teaching on baptism. Disciples of John the Baptist had moved to Ephesus only practising immersion as a sign of repentance. Paul knew that these disciples did not understand that faith was more than acknowledging sin and asking forgiveness. Salvation came from accepting Jesus as Messiah, Saviour and Lord. Baptism was an outward sign of a public confession of that reality. When a believer accepted Jesus as Saviour and Lord, he/she received God's acknowledgment and assurance by gracing the believer with his Spirit. Paul saw to it that the heresy was stopped immediately.

Ephesus was no small city and not without considerable influence. By Paul's time, the city was the capital of the region, and vied with Rome as the largest city of the Roman Empire. Ephesus was wonderfully situated for commerce at the mouth of the Cayster River where it met the

Mediterranean. In Paul's time the port welcomed traders from all the world. At Harbour Street, a colonnaded avenue led directly to the great theatre accommodating 25,000 spectators to Greek dramas and Roman gladiatorial events.

More important than the great theatre to the Ephesian residents was the striking Temple of Artemis, once recognized as among the Seven Wonders of the Ancient World. Artemis, according to Ephesian myth, was the mother goddess who gave birth to the city. Artemis (Diana to Romans) was depicted by a tall maternal idol featuring many breasts (some say bull's testicles) that symbolized fertility and the myth of birthing the ancient city. The original temple was completed in 550 BC, destroyed by conflict in 356 BC and rebuilt.

That desecration still haunted the psyche of Ephesians when Paul arrive there. Woe to those who haboured thoughts of damaging Artemis' presence in the city! Paul quickly found that edginess to be a factor in his Ephesian ministry.

In AD 431, most of the church bishops held an Ecumenical Council in Ephesus at the "double" church of Mary. These pastor-leaders formulated some doctrines which have resided in parts of the church ever since, although some Christians repudiate some of their decisions. Regrettably, as church history developed, ecclesiastical traditions often trumped biblical principles and scriptural authority.

Target One:
Inadequate Theology

By the time Paul and Luke arrived in Ephesus, as noted, some inadequate versions of the Gospel had taken root. Disciples of John "the Baptist" persuaded a number of the citizenry to repent and be baptized. This was once the doing of Apollos who recently had appeared in Corinth and had been corrected. Christian faith was much more than repentances, Paul told the cult of John members. They did not have the full gospel, which included trust in Jesus as Lord, Son of God, Saviour. This faith was measured by a belief that Jesus was crucified as atonement for human sin, was resurrected, ascended to heaven and sent the Holy Spirit to believers. The cult members then allowed Paul to place hands of anointing on them and the group members received the Holy Spirit. As Paul later described his mission, "I have declared to both Jews and Greeks that they must turn to God in repentance *and* have faith in the Lord Jesus."[130]

From his Ephesian almost three-year hiatus, Paul also sought to deal with challenges in other needful churches. He was no longer in Corinth in person, so he sent letters, at least one, from Ephesus to Corinth. His second letter to Corinth may have emanated from Philippi. No one knows for certain. Paul's ministry was not only making disciples but also maturing them in their faith.

---

[130] Acts 20:21

Target Two:
Share the Gospel in the Synagogue

Paul returned to a God-given strategy to share his Good News with Jews. They would be the first to hear that Messiah had finally arrived. So, for three intensive months the Apostle "boldly" shared his faith, experiences and exegesis of the Hebrew scriptures with them.

Evidently, Ephesus had only one synagogue but its membership numbers are unknown. After three months, when resistance grew into rejection, Paul leased a lecture hall in which to present his faith to the general public, including some Jews who liked what he had to say.

The hall may have belonged to someone interested in public debate, or it may have been named after a local Ephesian. Paul's ministry centred in this facility for two more years. He was in Ephesus for a total of three years.[131]

Target Three:
Work Where People Will Listen

Luke described Paul's detractors as obstinate and maligners of "The Way." No doubt that did not surprise Paul. He was announcing Jesus and his followers as "The Way." The subtlety in the description would anger many Jews

---

[131] Acts 20:31

because the term "way" referred to *halakah*, a Jewish term for "walking with God."

Now Paul had declared Jesus to be the way. Had not Jesus declared himself to be "the way (*halakah*), the truth and the life?"[132] Understandably, this was too much of a C-change for Jews who felt threatened by Jesus as Messiah. U-turns imply we are going the wrong way.

The strongest voices, if not the majority, in the synagogue carried the day, forcing Paul to call another mission strategy into play. The Apostle knew that there was no point in addressing those who were deaf to his message. Jesus told his disciples the same thing: "if anyone will not welcome you or listen to your words, shake the dust off your feet when you leave that home or town."[133] Share your faith with those who will appreciate it.

Evidently, Ephesus' Hall of Tyrannus to which Paul relocated, allowed a wider audience much more interested in accepting his teaching. Paul's "disciples" joined him daily for two more years. Together they strengthened the Gospel ministry.

Luke describes the new learners as Jews and Greeks[134] who lived in the province of Asia. Could that have meant the circle of what later has been called "The Seven

---

[132] John 14:6

[133] Matthew 10:14

[134] Acts 19:10

Churches?" That would include Ephesus, Smyrna, Sardis, Thyatira, Pergamum, Philadelphia and Laodicea.

Adjacent to these seven Asia Minor cities would be Hierapolis (Apollo's sacred city) and Colossae. Paul seems not to have visited any of these other communities, so perhaps those attending the evangelism classes of Paul at Tyrannus Hall, returned home to share their faith.

The consequence of such speculation would suggest believers in these communities formed into local bodies of Christ, community churches. Paul credits Epaphras[135] (Epaphroditus) as the instigator of teaching the Good News in Colossae.

A Discreet Time to Withdraw

Paul and his disciples made such headway in their mission that the trade of local idol-makers suffered a recession. The new faith badly hurt the profit margins of craftsmen who sculpted statuettes of Artemis. Artisans were regulated, so the entire guild of artisans, supported by other guilds in the city, created no small stir in Ephesus. Since guilds each had patron deities, this fall-off in sales meant disrespect of the city's patron guardian, Artemis.

Translation: "not only will we artists lose revenue but the fertility influences of Artemis may affect our city's sex life!" The populace understood the trickle down

---

[135] Colossians 1:7

economics of this situation and gravitated to the general meeting call by the silversmiths in Ephesus' Great Theatre. The anti-Paul rally is described by Luke as a city "in uproar."[136]

Paul was ready to defend his cause, especially when two Macedonian aides were seized. However, others of Paul's supporters cautioned him to not enter the fray. Sympathetic city officials who befriended Paul texted him to stay away. Intermediaries prevailed.

The city clerk advised that the courts could handle the Paul situation if charges were levelled against him. The clerk calmed the crowd. The rioters dispersed on a threat of their own breaking the peace. Paul got the message, gave his blessing to the believers and said good-bye. He sought to strengthen believers in Greece, and headed to Jerusalem.

Stopping Places

Was Paul driven, drawn or led? Maybe he was a mixture of all three descriptions. After the kerfuffle in Ephesus Paul returned to Macedonia, Philippi, probably Berea and Thessalonica. Several faithful new disciples, some from Macedonia, some from Asia Minor accompanied Paul, Timothy and Luke on this journey of shoring up the churches. After three months of encouraging the believers in these areas, he intended to visit Syria but was blocked by a

---

[136] Acts 19:29

cabal of Jewish malicious bullies. He learned of the plot against him, foiled it, and planned a rendezvous at Troas with leaders from various churches.

Luke helps us understand the disquiet going on inside Paul. We watch him wondering what to do next. This was a repeat of his being stymied before God's revelation to him to lead a mission into Europe. The safest choice he had after Ephesus was to revisit former sites of mission victories when his declaration of the Gospel fell on many receptive ears. At this point Paul was more drawn than driven.

Jerusalem became a magnet for him and he knew it would lead to trouble. Luke records Paul meeting with church leaders in various ports between Macedonia and Caesarea. Luke describes these rendezvous in a way that reveals viable churches in Cyprus, Troas, Assos, Mitylene, Tyre, Ptolmais and Caesarea. The Apostle forewarned them all that they would not likely see him again. Once back in Caesarea, Paul commented on his own future: "I am ready not only to be bound, but also to die in Jerusalem for the name of the Lord Jesus."[137]

As soon as Paul arrived at Caesarea, he journeyed to Philip's house. Previously, Philip was described as a deacon. Now Luke describes him as an evangelist. After resting at Philip's home, and without doubt, narrating the resulting work of the Gospel bearers in Greece, Macedonia and Asia Minor, the Apostle climbed the road to Jerusalem. His host in

---

[137] Acts 21:13

87

the holy city was Mnason, a Cypriot who was an early convert under the ministry of Barnabas, Mark and Saul. A day later, Paul conferred with James and other elders of the Jerusalem church, reporting on and accounting for his commission. It was a great report – thousands of converts.

The Jerusalem church leaders also gave Paul advice. To show that he had not forsaken the law of Moses or the habits of Jews, they urged him to prepare adequately to enter the Temple. These leaders knew the criticisms of and gossip about Paul in the various meeting places of the city. They told him to join four others who had made a vow, to shave his head, to ritually purify himself in a *mikveh* (immersion vat) by the Temple steps, and make a suitable Temple offering. He then planned to bring the gifts he had brought with him from Christians abroad to the Jerusalem church.

CHAPTER SEVEN
Jerusalem and Caesarea

The Apostle received an appallingly abrasive answer at Jerusalem's Temple complex. His detractors were Jews from Asia Minor, probably from Thessalonica and other locales where adversaries roundly rebuffed Paul's Gospel message that Jesus was the Messiah they had waited for, that he was the Son of God, was crucified for the sins of all, had risen from the grave and was now seated at God's place of honour in the heavens.

These critics accused Paul of defiling the Temple by bringing a Greek from Ephesus into the sacred centre of their faith (he did not do this). To Jews, this was an abomination akin to the act of sacrificing a pig on the holy altar, just as Antiochus Epiphanes had done two centuries earlier.

A riot broke out, the city gates were closed and

Roman soldiers saved Paul from an ignominious death by beating. They took him to the garrison (the Praetorium or Antonio) for his protection. After identifying himself as a Jew and as a Roman citizen, the garrison commander gave Paul leave to speak. Paul then offered his testimony of conversion and as a follower of Jesus. Paul followed Jesus' command to "go and make disciples." He saw every situation to be one in which he could follow Jesus' directives.

Paul's Roman citizenship saved him from imminent death that day. A divine night vision assured Paul he would live to testify in Rome. Hearing of a Sanhedrin plot to dispatch Paul, Roman officers whisked Paul away to the safety of the Roman coastal administrative centre at Caesarea Maritima.

Paul was detained for two years in Caesarea. The governor rejected some of the Jewish charges against him and allowed Paul to defend himself against those charges. He enjoyed some privileges. Governor Felix permitted Paul regular visitors, some limited freedom and many opportunities to declare his faith, not only to the governor himself, but to anyone and everyone within the range of his persuasive preaching. Felix' successor, Festus, kept Paul a prisoner to appease the Sanhedrin.

Paul would have to get used to his new limited freedom. Sent to Rome, he managed to greet friends along the way in various ports where the Centurion Julius had found prisoner galleys with passage to Rome. Paul's friends supplied Paul and Luke with provisions for their arduous late autumn journey. When the gales grew in magnitude Paul could not resist warning Julius and the sailors of impending catastrophe. Sailors would not heed the advice of someone they believed was an inexperienced "landlubber." Neither would Julius, so Paul's strong caution from travel experience fell on deaf ears. Just as Paul told them all, the ship broke up – but not before Paul gave a testimony about the power of God to save everyone.

CHAPTER EIGHT
Malta and Rome

Citizens of Malta must have scratched their heads to see all 276 survivors of the shipwreck wade ashore in what is now dubbed St. Paul's Bay on Malta's northwest shore. Moreover, when they helped the survivors, they treated them with genuine hospitality. Paul responded with Christian grace and was an agent in the healing of a Maltese official's father. This led to other healings. The impression has lasted. Today, Malta is filled with devout believers and 80% of them worship each Sunday in local churches.

Three months later Julius, Paul and Luke sailed for Syracuse in Sicily, then to Rhegium near the Messina Straits, and on to Puteoli (modern Anzio) on mainland Italy. A church already existed in that community and some of its members provided hospitality to Luke and Paul for a week.

No doubt this was a mutual heartening, Paul shored up the faith of the believers and the believers shared their love with Paul.

The aforementioned theme of Acts 2:42–47 showed itself in that church. Paul had earlier written to Roman believers, spelling out his comprehensive faith to them as in the letter to the Romans. Without doubt, therefore, Paul did not have to introduce himself to the Puteoli congregation.

Paul did not need to introduce himself to Roman Christians either. He wrote a letter to Rome, probably from Corinth, detailing his beliefs. Moreover, the church in Rome began probably as early as the pilgrims returned after Pentecost when Jews from Rome attended the rites of *Shavuot* in Jerusalem.[138] Numerous Jews lived in Jerusalem, were expelled, and returned when the persecutions diminished. Aquila and Priscilla came from Rome during this time, sojourned in Corinth, then Ephesus, and re-emerged in Rome by the time Paul penned his letter to the Romans.

Many Jews received the gospel gladly. They shared it with Gentiles as Peter prophesied on *Shavuot* at the *Ophel* in Jerusalem.[139] But more than the *Shavuot* visitors to the *Ophel* in Jerusalem told the story to Roman citizens. The Good News also came by way of traders, merchants, courtiers, army personnel and wayfarers all of whom had

---

[138] Acts 2:10

[139] Acts 2:39

heard about Jesus in ports around the Mediterranean. They could not stop gossiping about it. So Rome was a mixture of Jews and Gentiles living somewhat comfortably together in the fledgling, mushrooming Roman congregation.

Roman believers, concerned perhaps about the many faith counterfeits travelling Rome's Empire, needed affirmation that Paul was the real thing.

As noted, his answer to them took the form of a letter in which he first sent greetings, advised them that he was a legitimate Apostle, and identified himself being connected to some people well-known to them in the congregation. Some call that letter "The Fifth Gospel," because it so carefully crystallizes the essence of the Christian faith. The book of Romans is evidence that Paul not only made disciples by preaching, but also exercised his ministry in forming the theology of the Church.

This letter is much unlike the corrective epistles that Paul found necessary to send to Galatia, Ephesus, Corinth, Thessalonica and Colossae. Romans is Paul's synthesis of the Christian faith, describing the grace of God, the universal aspects of Christian faith for Jews and non-Jews, the need for, and affirmation of Jesus' atonement for sin, the place of faith/trust in the salvation process (justification), the adoption of all converts in the family of God, and the work of the Holy Spirit in sanctifying believers.

Rome may also have been the source of Paul's letters to various churches, such as Ephesus, Colossae and

Philippians. What does one do in prison to keep alert but send signals to one's friends? Paul was well-situated to help these churches who, like him, were going through difficulties of one sort or another.

Once in Rome Paul continued to declare his knowledge of God's work in Jesus. Although chained, Paul was able to live in a rented house[140] and invite neighbours in to hear him "explain and declare to them the kingdom of God and try to convince them about Jesus from the Law of Moses and from the Prophets."[141] The results both then and now, are the same. Some believed. Some were unconvinced. Luke's last word was, "Boldly, and without hindrance, he preached the kingdom of God and taught about the Lord Jesus Christ."[142]

What happened to Paul? He died "with his boots on," as moderns might say. Perhaps Luke did too. Tradition, if not fact, says he was beheaded by Romans soldiers. Facts may differ. However, tradition, for what it is worth, proposes that after Paul's beheading in AD 65, he was buried in the family tomb of a devout Roman noblewoman, Matrona Lucilla. Only God knows. God also knows that he was faithful to the end in sharing his faith with the world.

Over the next 250 years, many declarers of the Word

---

[140] Acts 28:30

[141] Acts 28:23

[142] Acts 28:31

of God met fates similar to that of Paul. As Tertullian said, "the blood of the martyrs is the seed of the church."

PART II

Personal Factors

CHAPTER NINE

Basic Principles in the Apostle's Life

Paul the missionary, Apostle extraordinaire, at first indication, demonstrated a dedicated and unique sense of direction. He threw himself into whatever was his aim, and gave all his vigour to it. When he was a persecutor of the Way, he undertook it passionately and with conviction. Such is far too casual an analysis of Paul's mission and thrust.

When a reader takes a second look, however, the observer may note how Paul displayed significant signs of insecurity and confusion. E. P Sanders, in assessing Paul's strategies and mission, points out how differently the writer of Acts sees Paul's task from how Paul sees his own assignment from God.

The author of Acts and Paul disagreed fundamentally about his mission. Acts sees Paul as first of all apostle to the Jews of the Greek-speaking Diaspora. Paul regarded himself, however as an apostle to the Gentiles. So he describes himself [Romans 1: 5; 1: 13–15; 11:13], and accordingly he describes his converts as former pagans: the Thessalonians had turned from God from idols (1 Thess. 1:9); the Galatians had formerly worshipped "being which are not gods" (Gal. 4:8); the Corinthians had worshipped dumb idols (1 Cor. 12:2, cf. 6: 9-11); the Philippians were not circumcised (Phil 3:2).[143]

Sanders' portrayal of Paul for being confused about his assignment may be overstating his case. From his first encounter with Christians in Antioch, he was exposed to both Jews and Gentiles. Among the first "missionaries" were those coming to Antioch from Cyprus to tell that God's love extended to Gentiles also. "The Lord's hand was with them,"[144] as the scripture records the story. Paul, still called Saul, must have observed this personally and was influenced by it. When Barnabas arrived to observe what had happened in Antioch among non-Jews, "he saw the evidence of the grace of God."[145]

---

[143] Sanders, E. P. Paul. p. 19.

[144] Acts 11: 21.

[145] Acts 11: 23.

1. Paul Knowing Himself

Apart from his own experience on the Damascus Road, and the influence of the gracious Ananias who ministered to him in kindness and instruction following his conversion, Saul (Paul) must have observed the happy report of God's ministry in Cyprus. Moreover, Barnabas' ministry of encouragement[146] would have encouraged him also. The sense of humility exuded by Barnabas may have touched Paul's life.

Not long afterward we read that he became known as Paul.[147] His arrogance on the road to Damascus was gone, and he began to show a demeanour which reflected much more humility in his life.[148] His former kingly name, Saul, reflected Israel's pride and regal aspects; his latter name, Paul, meant "little" and he soon declared he was "less than the least of all saints."[149] As Peter wrote, "All of you must put on the apron of humility, to serve one another; for the scripture says, 'God resists the proud, but shows favour to

---

[146] Ibid.

[147] Acts 13: 9.

[148] Philippians 2: 1–11.

[149] Ephesians 3: 8.

the humble.'"[150] William Ramsay places little importance on the meaning of the names. Saul was a Jewish name, he noted. Paul was a Roman name. Ramsay argues that he simply used a different name to approach different audiences. Citing Paul's note to Corinth, Ramsay proposed:

> To the Jews I made myself a Jew that I might gain Jews; to them that are under the law (though not myself under the law); to them that are without the law as without the law; I am become all things to all men; and I do all for the Gospel's sake." We cannot doubt that the man who wrote so to the Corinthians replied to the questions of Sergius Paulus, by designating himself as a Roman, born at Tarsus, and named Paul. By a marvellous stroke of historic brevity, the author sets before us the past and the present in simple words: "Then Saul, otherwise Paul, fixed his eyes on him and said . . .[151]

The change in names coincided with a change from his own former arrogance as a persecutor into a new kind of humble daily living. Such humility quickly enabled Paul to put other people ahead of himself. He wrote to his "charges" in Philippi, "In humility consider others better than yourselves." One writer observed that "Paul . . . regarded himself as moulded by the lowliness of the crucified Christ

---

[150] 1 Peter 5:5 (TEV)

[151] Acts 13: 9; Ramsay, William M. St. Paul the Traveller and the Roman Citizen., pp. 81–83.

and – proleptically – by the power of the risen Christ (cf. esp. 2 Cor. 4: 10–11; Phil. 3: 10)."[152]

Dr. Coggan underlined this humility of Paul by phrasing it in alternate words. He simply said that Paul got "out of the way"[153] so as not to attract attention to himself. He redirected the attention to Christ.

> This is true of Paul, preacher, writer, Christian communicator. Indeed, it was the major reason for his success in these spheres. It was in proportion as he "got out of the way" that success, in the deepest meaning of that misused word, attended his work. As a man infinitely indebted to Christ, it was his first care "not to get in the way." This cannot have been easy for a man built on such ample proportions. A forceful, dynamic, sometimes abrasive character is not readily hidden. The secret – and he learned it the hard way and by no means always at once – was to "die daily" (1 Corinthians 15: 31). A daily recognition of himself as having died "to the appeal of the power of sin," but being "alive and sensitive to the call of Jesus Christ our Lord" (Romans 6:11).[154]

In an essay on *Humility and Self-Denial* of Jesus and Paul, Christian Wolff discusses four areas of commonality

---

[152] Christian Wolff in Wedderburn, A. J. M. (ed.). Paul and Jesus: Collected Essays. pp. 145–160.

[153] Coggan, Donald. Paul: Portrait of a Revolutionary, p. 223, 224.

[154] Ibid.

between Paul and his Lord. They were (1) deprivation; (2) renunciation of marriage; (3) humble service; and (4) suffering persecution.[155] These were prompted more by the intensity and immediacy of their individual missions. In Paul's instance, renunciation of marriage and suffering persecution were also connected to his sense of the end of the age.

Renunciations of marriage and suffering persecution are not necessarily requirements of someone making disciples. However, in these instances they helped. Neither Jesus nor Paul were encumbered by family responsibilities. Both were free to travel without restriction. The absence of family was met in part by the new family of believers.

Jesus knew he was the "beloved" of God.[156] Paul knew he had met Christ and had been confirmed by him as an apostle of Christ's love.[157] In knowing Christ, Paul came to know himself. He saw the qualities which God had given him as grace-gifts and he accepted them as gifts for God's service and not for merit or boasting. "For by the grace given me I say to every one of you: Do not think of yourself more highly than you ought, but rather think of yourself with sober judgment in accordance with the measure of faith God has

---

[155] Wedderburn, A. J. M. (ed.). op. cit., p. 160.

[156] Mark 1: 11.

[157] Galatians 1: 1.

given you."[158] That was Paul's clue to see himself as God saw him and to encourage other believers to see how God had likewise given them grace-gifts of service.

A. M. Hunter noted similarities and differences in Jesus and Paul. In some ways, Hunter sees no comparison. But "the same saving act of God is the theme of both gospels and epistles."[159]

> On their essential views of sin and salvation, Jesus and Paul are at one. Yet one decisive difference there is between them, and none realize it better than Paul. Jesus knew himself to be the Christ (or Messiah) of God and his only Son. Paul is the servant and envoy of this Christ. He is the Apostle: Jesus is his Lord, and his the only name given under heaven whereby men may be saved.[160]

2. Faith Factors in Paul's Mission Action

Paul's mission trust can hardly be understood without recognizing the degree to which Paul's faith in Christ propelled him into his apostolate. In an additional essay in Wedderburn's collection of essays, Christian Wolff comments on the surety of faith Paul had about Christ. This was the foundation for Paul's mission ventures. He was

---

[158] Romans 12: 3.

[159] Hunter, A. M. The Fifth Evangelist, p. 5.

[160] Ibid.

rooted in the saving work of Christ upon the cross.[161] Paul had been taught by the Spirit.[162] Paul had a clear sense of his personal justification and reconciliation with God, against whose Kingdom he had railed in his own spiritual blindness.[163] Paul clearly saw himself as a divinely-appointed ambassador of Christ's purposes.[164]

Alexander Wedderburn, in another essay contribution to the collection he edited, underlines that Paul was especially rooted in his belief in the resurrection of Jesus. "For Paul . . . Jesus' life and death seemed of no value without their vindication in his resurrection; thus he declares that 'if Christ had not been raised, our faith is void.'"[165]

The theme of resurrection dominated Paul's faith system. Father Murphy-O'Connor writes about Paul's encounter with the risen Christ and of the grace given to understand that God "was pleased . . . to reveal his Son to me."[166]

Paul now knew with the inescapable conviction of

---

[161] Wedderburn, A. J. M. (ed.). op cit., p. 90.

[162] Wedderburn, A. J. M. (ed.) op. cit. pp. 92.

[163] Ibid.

[164] Wedderburn, A. J. M. (ed.). op. cit., p. 94.

[165] Wedderburn, A. J. M. (ed.). op. cit., p. 178.

[166] Galatians 1:16.

direct experience that the Jesus who had been crucified under Pontius Pilate was alive. The resurrection which he had contemptuously dismissed was a fact, as undeniable as his own reality. He knew that Jesus now existed on another plane. This recognition is all that was necessary to his conversion, because it completely transformed his value system.[167]

The theme of Paul's work is reflected in the familiar words, "Christ has died. Christ is risen. Christ will come again." Such theological convictions affected the purpose of Paul's mission, the scope of it, the revisions of God's revelations and the intensity with which Paul undertook his witness. In a sense, as a unique individual, Paul was "his own person," but in reality he understood that in every thought, word or deed he was not his own but "bought with a price."[168]

3. Paul the Revolutionary

Archbishop Donald Coggan calls Paul a revolutionary. He was part of the Pharisee movement which had insisted on maintaining the traditional *Torah* regulations, sometimes abandoned by a lax Jewish society.[169] The

---

[167] Murphy-O'Connor, Jerome. Paul: A Critical Life. p. 78.

[168] 1 Corinthians 6: 20.

[169] Coggan, Donald. op. cit., p. 25.

Pharisees existed to demonstrate by their separateness that God's laws should be fully observed. That they went to extreme ends to show this by their meticulous tithing of herbs[170] does not detract from their revolutionary zeal. Jesus also mentioned their misguided zeal in attracting proselytes. "Woe to you, scribes and Pharisees, hypocrites! For you cross sea and land to make a single convert, and you make the new convert twice as much a child of hell as yourselves."[171]

Surely Paul's revolution was rooted in his dramatic conversion.[172] Usually, revolutionaries are created from one defining point in their lives. Paul's defining moment took place on the road to Damascus and he referred to it at least three times in his witness to others.[173]

> *And then it happened*! Let us not ask, too precisely, what "it" was. We may use psychological jargon if we will; it may help, it may not. We may posit the possibility that Saul had an epileptic fit. That may help some; it does not help me. Rather, let us beware the banality of seeking to explain the ways of God with men, the God who has as many ways of reaching our innermost beings with his love as he

---

[170] Luke 11:42.

[171] Matthew 23: 15

[172] Coggan, Donald. op. cit., p. 36.

[173] Acts 9: 1–19; Acts 22: 3–16; Acts 26: 12–18.

has of giving us different faces or different fingerprints. When God touches a man, turns him round in his tracks, looks into the eyes of the one who hitherto has been running away from him and crucifying the Son of God afresh, let us not try to explain that miracle of love and grace. Let us remember that, as there is a mystery surrounding the Being of God, so there is a mystery at the heart of his ways with men. Perhaps above every story of conversion we should write the warning, "Mystery! God at work."[174]

4. A Vocation by Which Paul
Could Answer his Higher Calling

Paul is described as a "tent maker."[175] It turned out to be a vocation by which he could answer his divine calling. Some booths or tents were made of linen and linen was a main commodity deriving from Tarsus.[176] Not only did this vocation acquaint Paul with Prisca and Aquila, but it may have given Paul a stronger bond with Lydia whose work is described as a seller of purple. Tent making also included leather, of course. The trade he learned may have helped Paul network with others. Tent makers had their own guild.[177]

---

[174] Ibid.

[175] Acts 18: 3.

[176] Murphy-O'Connor, Jerome. op. cit., pp. 86, 87.

[177] Ibid.

One wonders if this particular guild was especially helpful to Paul by its not having a patron pagan deity. If so, then Paul, Aquila, Prisca and Simon the Tanner[178] could avoid some of the issues of *kosher* eating and *halakah*. Thus tent making enabled Paul to both survive as a wage-earner and to file good linkages with fellow-workers around the Mediterranean.

> In terms of missionary strategy Paul chose wisely. He acquired a skill whose products many needed. It enabled him to travel widely, although it would never make him rich, even though he worked "night and day" (1Thessalonians 2: 9; 2 Thessalonians 3: 9.). It enabled him to survive, but only barely, because he never stayed in one place long enough to build up a stable clientele. As his ministry ate into his time, subsidies became necessary (Philippians 4: 15–16; 2 Corinthians 11: 9). But that day was still a long way in the future.[179]

5. The Open Connection
Between God's Spirit and Paul

Many observers of Paul have noticed his obvious reliance on God's Holy Spirit. The writer of Acts once used

---

[178] Acts 10: 6.

[179] Murphy-O'Connor, Jerome. op. cit., p. 88.

the phrase "the Spirit of Jesus"[180] but the meaning is the same. Paul looked for divine directions throughout his decision-making. He was frequently rewarded. A. M. Hunter argued that the Spirit connection to Paul was absolutely essential.

> To say that for many today the Holy Spirit is the most unreal part of their religion is to state the obvious. How very different it was in the glad springtime of our faith, as we may read in the Acts of the Apostles or the letters of Paul! Come to the New Testament with really fresh eyes, and you cannot mistake the enormous importance which the first Christians attached to the gift of the Holy Spirit as quite new, "a kind of 'wireless' between heaven and earth that was not there before." Because of this "anonymous third person" in their midst it was possible for every Christian church to be a sort of replica of the Galilean circle, with the living Christ still among them, messages still going and coming. As for Paul, you can no more understand his Christian teaching without the Holy Spirit than you can understand our modern civilization without the existence of electricity.[181]

Clearly, Paul enjoyed a personal relationship with the risen Christ that their mutual conversations amounted to thoughts bathed in prayer. Paul's Christ did not always give

---

[180] Acts 16: 7.

[181] Hunter, A. M. op. cit., pp. 88, 89.

111

him immediate answers to pleadings and requests. Sometimes the Lord's answer to Paul was more grace. "My grace is sufficient for you, for my power is made perfect in weakness."[182] The grace was very special to Paul who knew he had not merited God's favours.

F. F. Bruce linked this special relationship of Paul and Jesus to Paul's realization of knowing the exalted Christ.

> If, as has been said . . . "The empty tomb and the resurrection appearances mark the transition from the historical Jesus to the exalted Christ," it is implied that the exalted Christ is continuous and personally identical with the historic Jesus. This continuity and personal identity were maintained by Paul. While, however, the historic Jesus was known to him only by hearsay and tradition, he claimed a direct and profound personal acquaintance with the exalted Christ.[183]

6. Systematic Theological Thought

By his several letters and individual ministries, Paul set forth the first systematics for the church. He was wonderfully prepared for this theological synthesis by his vital awareness of Jewish and Roman law.[184] He may have

---

[182] 2 Corinthians 12: 9.

[183] Bruce, F. F. Paul: Apostle of the Free Spirit, p. 113.

[184] Johnson, Hubert Rex. Who Then Is Paul? pp. 30, 31.

absorbed his knowledge of the Cynics and Stoics in the local agora of Tarsus.[185]

Paul's orthodox theology has become the reference point of the larger church throughout the centuries since the time of Christ or his apostle, Paul. F. F. Bruce cites different eras of Christian life in which Pauline theology – whether correctly understood or not – became the plumb line for reform and correction. These included Augustine, Luther and the Reformation, the Wesleys and evangelical revival, and in this century, Barth and the theology of crisis.[186]

7. Ministry to and with People

This book began by asking what basics Paul used in helping to establish churches. Front and centre to the answers is that Paul did not see "the church" as an institution. He saw the church as people who had come to know Christ. This group of people was not androgynous but was certainly uniformly accepted by Paul's God through faith and grace. Without limit Paul notes that such believers "in Christ" were from every walk of life – ethnically diverse without preference, male and female, educated and unskilled, slave

---

[185] Ibid.

[186] Bruce, F. F. op. cit. pp. 470–473.

owner and slave.[187]

This remarkable acceptance on the part of Paul mirrored God's acceptance of those who in faith accepted his grace and were saved. How can one separate Paul's personal investment of his whole person from the ministry into which he gave himself? It can hardly be done. His example of a totally invested life is as large a model for establishing churches as any other method or pilot project.

F.F. Bruce reflected on Paul's personality:

> He was . . . sociable, gregarious. He delighted in the company of his fellows, both men and women. The most incredible feature in the Paul of popular mythology is his alleged misogyny. He treated women as persons: we recall his commendation of Phoebe, the deacon of the church in Cenchraea, who had shown herself a helper to him as to many others, or his appreciation of Euodia and Syntyche of Philippi who worked side by side with him in the gospel. The mainstream churches of Christendom, as they inch along towards a worthier recognition of the ministry of women, have some way to go yet before they come abreast of Paul.

The range of his friendship and the warmth of his affection are qualities which no attentive reader of his letters can miss. There are scores of people mentioned in the New Testament who are known to us, by name at least, simply

---

[187] Galatians 3:28; 1 Corinthians 12: 13; Romans 10: 12; Colossians 3: 11.

because they were friends of Paul. And in his friends he was able to call forth a devotion which knew no limits. Priscilla and Aquila risked their lives for him in a dangerous situation. Epaphroditus of Philippi overtaxed his strength and suffered an almost fatal illness in his anxiety to be of service to the imprisoned apostle. Timothy readily surrendered whatever personal ambitions he might have cherished in order to play the part of a son to Paul and help him in his missionary activity, showing a selfless concern for others that matched the apostle's own eagerness to spend and be spent.

Summary

Starting churches and establishing them require two different objectives. Nowhere do we read that Paul set out to start churches. He simply preached the gospel which the first missionaries called "the word of God."[188] Paul offered the word of God. The people who received it became the church.

This chapter has identified seven factors which created opportunities for "establishing" churches. *First*, Paul knew who he was. *Secondly*, the faith factors in Paul's life were conducive to his successful ministry. *Thirdly*, Paul had a revolutionary spirit within him. *Fourthly*, Paul used a vocation by which he could satisfy his divine calling. *Fifthly*, he was well-connected with God's Spirit. *Sixthly*, Paul created a systematic approach to faith which gave the early

---

[188] Acts 3: 5.

churches a paradigm for faith and action. *Seventhly*, Paul had a "hands-on" ministry to individuals who made up the larger faith communities called "churches."

Establishing churches is a different matter than commencing them. When Paul was advised to leave Berea, he left Silas and Timothy to help the Bereans become rooted in Christ. His letters to various churches over which he had some influence reflect his ministry of giving them correction and rootedness. Such churches required theological and moral schooling. They needed to know their sense of community (*koinonia*) with each other. Paul, by his personal counsel through visits and letters, provided this foundation for a future gospel witness.

Paul's letter to Colossae reflects the "establishing" nature of Paul's life work. "Just as you received Christ Jesus as Lord, continue to live in him, rooted and built up in him, strengthened in the faith as you were taught, and overflowing with thankfulness."[189]

---

[189] Colossians 2: 6, 7.

CHAPTER TEN

Leadership Skills:
Key Principles *in* Leadership *for* Church Growth

The church was born on *Shavuot*, some seven weeks after Jesus was crucified, and rose from the dead. When the baby was born, God immediately filled her tender lungs with his breath. In God's good plan the birthing took place in Jerusalem – likely at the *Ophel*, the Temple's south wall and stairs, where male pilgrims always congregated for purification purposes before entering the Temple Mount for their prayers and sacrifices. The timing and the location ensured that a maximum number of Jews and God-fearers would hear and receive the good news of Jesus as God's anointed one and saviour of the world.

Some three thousand of the several thousand Jewish and God-fearer pilgrims who had prepared themselves to fellowship with God in their acts of devotion received the news with acceptance and endorsement. They believed. They repented. They were baptized in water and by the Spirit. They fellowshipped with the disciples and other believers. Immediately they took instruction in faith and life matters. As Acts records the story, "They devoted themselves to the apostle's teaching and fellowship, to the breaking of bread and the prayers."[190]

Since so many of them came from abroad[191] for the festival of first fruits, they soon returned to their native soils and shared their newly-found faith with family and friends. Their first commitment was not to start a church but to "gossip the gospel." One cannot imagine them telling their friends, "Let's start a church." They probably had no concept of an organized "church," only of a fellowship of believers. The *ekklesia* followed their witness about Jesus, and likely happened without any intention on their parts.

The summary of what happened on Pentecost and of its subsequent activities is provided in Acts. First,[192] they welcomed the message, repented, believed in Jesus' messiahship, crucifixion and resurrection, then sought instruction and fellowship with other believers through "the breaking of bread." Acts does not elaborate on "the breaking

---

[190] Acts 2:42.

[191] Acts 2:8 ff.

[192] Acts 2:42 ff.

of bread," but it could refer to common meals[193] or to the Eucharist. There followed "signs and wonders," a sense of wonderment, a sharing of possessions and common praise "with glad and generous hearts."[194] The most telling comment of this activity was that "day by day the Lord added to their number those who were being saved."[195]

Therein is a partial model for church growth. Add to that the testimony of Acts in its remaining chapters, a host of instructions, encouragements, admonitions and principles in the epistles and the model is much more complete. What follows is extrapolated from these biblical sources as well as commentary from a variety of modern church growth "experts."

The following offering is divided between spiritual and natural gifts for leadership modelling in kingdom expansion. The qualities are not necessarily listed in order of importance. Obviously no individual possesses them all; God, apparently has allowed us many deficiencies in order that we be interdependent[196] with each other.[197] The telling phrase which delineates this growth as kingdom-oriented is

---

[193] Acts 2:46.

[194] Acts 2:47.

[195] Ibid.

[196] 1 Corinthians 3:9.

[197] Romans 12:3–8; 1 Corinthians 12:26; Ephesians 2:20, 21.

that "The Lord added to their number."[198] In his first letter to Corinth, Paul paraphrased the same principle: "God gave the growth."[199]

Before offering the main content of this analysis, the writer points to an important insight from one of the earliest proponents of the church growth movement. C. Peter Wagner notes that he has changed his mind on a number of issues related to that movement. He obviously heard Samuel Escobar's complaint that this movement took little account of justice and economic issues.[200]

Others also contributed to Wagner's new insights.[201] Raymond J. Bakke reviewed an earlier work of Wagner and observed, "It's been a long time since I read a significant work on ecclesiology or missiology that never once mentioned the kingdom . . ."[202] Justice C. Anderson of Southwestern Baptist Theological Seminary, wrote, "Perhaps the Church Growth School needs a stronger emphasis on the kingdom concept."[203] The biggest issue in the early days of the church growth movement was growth for its own sake.

---

[198] Acts 2:47.

[199] 1 Corinthians 3:6.

[200] Wagner, Peter. Church Growth and the Whole Gospel., p. xii.

[201] Ibid.

[202] Wagner, Peter. op cit., p. 2.

[203] Ibid.

Now Wagner confesses that the movement often failed to understand that the kingdom (*basileia*,[204] "royal power," "dominion") of God ought to have been its first priority. He admits,

> Appearing among all this was the theme that the kingdom of God had already begun in America. As H. R. Niebuhr tells us, 'The kingdom of the Lord was a human possession . . . in particular the kingdom of the Anglo-Saxon race, which is destined to bring light to the gentiles by means of lamps manufactured in America.'[205]

I follow the views of those scholars who see a partial identification of the church with the kingdom of God. I agree with George Ladd, who says, "If the dynamic concept of the kingdom is correct, it is never to be identified with the church . . . The kingdom is the rule of God; the church is a society of men." The church should totally reflect the lifestyle of the kingdom but as we are painfully aware, it does not. While most Christians I know do acknowledge Jesus as their Lord and seriously try to live lives that would be a credit to the kingdom of God, few, if any fully accomplish it, and they are embarrassed by their failure. The church even includes on its rolls some extremely nominal members who do not attend worship services, who use the Lord's name in vain, who do not tithe their income, who succumb to the lust of the flesh, the lust of the eyes and the pride of

---

[204] Wagner, Peter. op. cit., p. 4.

[205] Wagner, Peter. op. cit. p. 3.

121

life, who get drunk, who have little concern for the poor, and, who if it were legal, would keep slaves. No, the church cannot be identified with the kingdom one-on-one.

But this same church is described in the Bible as the bride of Christ, the household of God. Its members are called to be saints (Rom. 1:1). It is a "chosen race, a royal priesthood, a holy nation, God's own people" (1 Pet 2:9 RSV). This is kingdom language. It would be a mistake to divorce the church entirely from the kingdom. Ladd argues that those who received Jesus' preaching of the kingdom were viewed as inheritors of the future kingdom but also "as the people of the kingdom in the present, and, therefore, in some sense of the word, a church." I like the way Howard Snyder describes the church as "a charismatic community and God's people, his kingdom of priests . . . the community of the king." The kingdom creates the church, not vice versa.[206]

Kingdom and Spirit are fundamental to understanding the nature of the church. The church exists only under the aegis of the kingdom of God. The church, the body of Christ, finds its source unity, power and direction from God's Holy Spirit.[207]

Therefore, the first qualities which leaders require for proper church growth are those of the Spirit. Following are some 10 – many more, no doubt – spiritual qualities

---

[206] Wagner, Peter. op cit., p. 39

[207] Ephesians 4:4.

122

which serve church leadership well. Since they cannot likely be found in any one person, the whole church may be gifted together in a greater way than in the sum of the several spiritual parts amid the membership.

A. Spiritual Qualities

1. A Conviction of Call

The apostle Paul had a clear sense of election to his apostolic office.[208] His "calling" was punctuated by virtual visions in which he was met by his Lord on the road to Damascus,[209] then during various dire straits in which God gave him confirmation.[210] Jeremiah too, knew that God had called him to be a prophetic voice.[211] He wrestled with God on this calling[212] but he knew for a fact that prophecy was God's unique will for him.[213]

Some who are "called" for God's service may have such clear directions from the Lord but many other leaders

---

[208] 1 Corinthians 1:1

[209] Acts 9:3–5; Acts 22:6–9; Acts 26:12:–18

[210] Acts 16:9; Acts 23:11.

[211] Jeremiah 1:5.

[212] Jeremiah 1:6.

[213] Jeremiah 1:7, 8.

sense their calling through circumstances of opened doors or closed opportunities. Charles Colson discovered this in prison. "God builds his church in the most unlikely ways and places, stirring the convictions of the heart, bringing men and women to the knowledge of sin, to repentance, to the Saviour himself – and knitting them together in the body," he wrote.[214]

Bill Hybels, a model in church growth leadership as demonstrated by the Willow Creek phenomenon in Illinois, found his calling in gradual degrees of service. He soon discovered he was gifted to preach – and so he did.

> I discovered I had the spiritual gifts of preaching and teaching – and at the same time. I'd never heard of spiritual gifts! But the kids not only were listening, but also they were being impacted by the Word of God as it came off the page through my lips . . . I was amazed that this rather unconventional exercise – standing there with the Bible and talking about it – had such power for good, for Christ, in the lives of people.[215]

Similarly, while some ministry prospects want to believe they have a call to a certain ministry, trial and error provide the answer that they must adjust to enrolling in a

---

[214] Colson, Charles. A Dangerous Grace., p. 7.

[215] Hybels, Bill, Briscoe, Stuart and Robinson, Haddon. op. cit. p. 11.

much different ministry than they first envisioned. Paul Stevens explained that he wanted to be a pastor but after years of agonizing felt led to become a teaching leader in another denomination.

> A few years ago my determination and reflection drove me to take up the hammer and saw to work as a carpenter for five years. By becoming a tentmaker like Aquila and Priscilla (Acts 18:1–3) I was trying to rediscover the lay vocation in society. I learned some important lessons relating to neighbours and trying to raise a family. If Christianity does not relate to the realities of Monday to Saturday as experienced by the ordinary church member, then it is just another religion. The tentmaking experience drove me back into pastoral ministry again and eventually into theological education where I teach the theology of work, vocation, and ministry for the laity.[216]

Whatever God's plan is for any individual, the person must seek the place of service which God has for her or him. God does not provide square pegs for round holes. His plan is for the parts to fit together[217] so as to created maximum service for his kingdom work. Church growth requires in its leaders an assurance that they serve in a capacity to which God has called them.

---

[216] Stevens, Paul and Collins, Phil. The Equipping Pastor. , p. xiv.

[217] Romans 8:28; Ephesians 2:21,22.

2. A Deep Faith in Christ

Leadership calls for an abiding faith in Christ. No leader can give away what he does not already possess. Stanley Jones wrote,

> If we are to be mature, we must get hold of a mature faith – or better, it must get hold of us. For the immaturities of our faith will soon show themselves in our actions and our attitudes. "The creed of today becomes the deed of tomorrow" . . . For *belief* is literally *by-lief*, *by life* – the things you live by. And if your belief is wrong, your life will be wrong.[218]

A deep faith in Christ is basic to Christian discipleship. Frank Harrington, former pastor of the growing Peachtree Presbyterian Church in Atlanta, asked his congregation one Christmas, "Why proclaim the gospel if there is no challenge for commitment? He [Jesus] has come not just to visit us but to occupy our hearts."[219]

When a leader has a deep faith in Christ he does not promote himself but becomes a channel of God's blessings to others. That was the Pauline principle of ministry. To a potentially schismatic situation in Philippi, Paul wrote to the effect that some selfish leaders "badmouthed" him but "What does it matter? Just this: that Christ is proclaimed in every

---

[218] Jones, Stanley E. Christian Maturity. p. 3.

[219] Harrington, W. Frank. First Comes Faith. p., 67.

way, whether out of false motives or true; and in that I rejoice."[220]

Halford E. Luccock, the one-time homiletics professor at Yale Divinity School, emphasized the necessity of a preacher's sure footing in God so as to allow God's grace to flow through him without drawing attention to himself.

> At an ordination service a few years ago the preacher who gave the charge to the young minister pleaded eloquently for consecration of mind and energy, and ended up with the exhortation, "Now go out and give to your preaching all that is in you." It was a fitting word for the occasion, persuasively spoken; yet it would be hard to conceive a better definition of just what preaching is *not*. It is not giving all that is in us; it is giving that which is not in us at all. It is the preacher presenting himself and all that he is and has as a channel for something that is not in him, the grace of God. The first words of the Bible are the first words of preaching: "in the beginning God."[221]

The Christian leader must have a deep rooted experience in Jesus Christ, the Lord. What he does not know personally he cannot transmit. But once knowing it experientially, he must allow that rootedness of God's grace be transmitted humbly through him. Good growth won't

---

[220] Philippians 1:18.

[221] Luccock, Halford E. In The Minister's Workshop., p. 11.

happen without that essential trust in Christ's work and words, or in discounting his instructions or teachings.

3. A Sense of God's Timing

Paul wrote to the Galatians about God's sense of timing. "When the fulness of time had come, God sent his Son."[222] The world had a common language – Greek. The world had a relatively peaceful existence under Roman rule. The world enjoyed safe travel and effective international communications. Jesus was born in a period when the world conditions provided maximum opportunity for Christ's mediating message and absolute atonement.

The book of Acts likewise shows its readers another instance of God's choice timing. God gave his Spirit at a time of festival when the Jewish world was focussing on Jerusalem during *Shavuot*. In this setting everyone who believed in Jesus as the messianic saviour became a missionary and messenger of God. The arrival of the Holy Spirit coincided with the maximum opportunity for new believers to disseminate their faith and spiritual discovery.

Was it God's timing that sent Aquila and Priscilla to Corinth from Rome? Leaders and churches must learn how to discern and appropriate God's time. Archbishop George Carey explained that a motor vehicle accident put him in the hospital and thus prevented him from chairing a meeting

---

[222] Galatians 4:4.

relating to changes in the church building. A lay chairman took over in lieu of the vicar. The meeting produced excellent results, suggesting that God had a better plan for the meeting than if George Carey had conducted it.[223]

Sometimes God opens doors as wide as can be and it is essential that the people of God sense that God wants them to act *now* and enter through them to the opportunity he has prepared for them. A plot of land becomes available. The location was not as planned. The money is not immediately available. Do God's people look seriously at whether their previous plans were not the right ones or if alternative money sources are available? There is no right answer in this hypothetical instance but the issue is sensitivity to God's timing. Is it now? Only the prayerful sensitivity of God's faithful people will produce the appropriate vision.

George Barna offered an example of a pastor whose new sense of vision opened his eyes to God's timing. The church mushroomed from 25 to 1,600 in six years. The pastor remarked,

> One of the chief lessons for me was discovering the difference between doing what the people expect a pastor to do and doing what God has called me to do . . .
> In my previous position I was carrying the mission without vision. Now, I'm pursuing the vision within

---

[223] Carey, George. The Church in the Market Place., pp. 81, 82.

the context of our mission to serve God.[224]

Jesus told his disciples to be on their watch. "You must be ready for the Son of Man is coming at an unexpected hour."[225] This reality applies to more than end times. It is a constant truth. God chooses when and where he discloses himself and his plans. The alert disciple of Jesus waits and listens for the breath of God to direct him.

4. A Place for Prayer; An Awareness of the Spirit's Leading

"Pray without ceasing"[226] does not mean that a Christian must be forever on his knees. It does mean that we need to be in constant communication with the Father to know what his Spirit has planned for us. McGavran applies that constraint to church planning and church growth. "Ideas must be clothed in flesh. A wonderful way to begin in prayer. If in any congregation a group were to pray and continue steadfastly in prayer that the church would grow, their church would grow."[227]

---

[224] Barna, George. The Power of Vision., pp. 77, 78.

[225] Luke 12:40

[226] 1 Thessalonians 5:17.

[227] McGavran, Donald A., and Arn, Win. How To Grow A Church, p. 177.

Following the day of Pentecost prayer was a mark of the initial church meetings.[228] The prayers entered into are not explained. Undoubtedly they included the regular prayers for the festival of *Shavuot*, prayers related to ritual cleansing, and the prayers of ascent for entering the Temple Mount. Since this group had acknowledged Jesus as Messiah and their Saviour, they likely recited messianic psalm prayers. Their prayers would be full of adoration and thanksgiving for the gospel disclosures.

Yet their petitions would also have included prayers for the completion of the kingdom and the salvation of unbelievers. Probably they prayed about specific friends and relatives whom they wanted to introduce, by God's Spirit, to the Father through his Son. Harold Percy wrote, "All of life is lived at the gate of heaven. Growing Christians are coming to understand that all of life is worship. For this we were created. In this, we find life."[229]

Obviously, a leader provided by God must spend significant time and place in God's counsel. Shirley Bentall reminded her readers that "The Father has given prayer to us."[230] She continued,

When Jesus came, he spoke about prayer with all the

---

[228] Acts 2:42.

[229] Percy, Harold. Following Jesus., p. 106.

[230] Bentall, Shirley. Discovering the Deep Places., p. 58.

authority and from the perspective of God the Father, who calls us to pray. He not only talked about prayer, he prayed himself, and he lived in a persistent attitude of prayer. His whole life was a prayer, and we are intended to learn about prayer from him.[231]

The baby church must have severely struggled as to how to interpret what had happened to her and what to do about it. Prayer was the most obvious response – to immerse herself in the counsel and direction of God. Bill Hybels said, "I can't tell you how much I miss going one day without God's voice whispering, *Go left, go right . . . Easy now, that person's tender. Yes, that's the way. Okay, good. Let's take on the next challenge.*"[232]

To make the next step the wrong step one only has to ignore fellowship with God. A leader or congregation that ignores divine direction is always susceptible to taking false footsteps and therefore the wrong path. Church growth is conditional on taking the right path.

Theologian Karl Barth reviewed the attitudes of Reformers about prayer. Adding his own insights, he noted:

We are not free to pray or not pray, nor to pray only when inclined, for prayer is not an activity which is natural to us. Prayer is grace, and we can expect this grace only from the Holy Spirit. This grace is with

---

[231] Ibid.

[232] Hybels, Bill. The God You're Looking For., p. 145.

God and his Word in Jesus Christ. If we accept this, and if we receive what God gives, then all is done, everything is in order, not as the result of our own good pleasure but in the freedom to obey him which is ours.[233]

5. An Openness to Others

Leadership in a church requires unqualified openness to others. Jesus set the theme; to him no one was an outsider. Judgmentalism is out-of-character to someone interested in helping others to come into fellowship with God through Christ. Leaders ought never to look only to someone's past or even his or her track record. A leader sees the potential in others, just as Jesus saw discipleship in Levi the "sinner," or Simon, the "zealot."

Hybels thinks this is crucial to ministry – at least to his ministry! He wrote,

> We can't win them if we don't know how they think, and we can't know how they think if we don't enter their world."[234]
> If we're going to speak with integrity to secular men and women, we need to work through two critical areas before we step into the pulpit . . . The first is to *understand the way they think* . . . The second prerequisite to effective preaching to non-Christians

---

[233] Barth, Karl. <u>Praying and Preaching</u>. pp. 22, 23.

[234] Hybels, Bill, Briscoe, Stuart, Robinson, Haddon. <u>op . cit</u>. p. 30.

is that we *like them*.[235]

Peter Wagner reminds his readers of how American Christians were so blinded to their own brand of nationalistic religion. "Appearing among all this," he wrote, "was the theme that the kingdom of God had already begun in America. As H. R. Niebuhr tells us, (previously quoted), 'The kingdom of the Lord was a human possession . . . in particular the kingdom of the Anglo-Saxon race, which is destined to bring light to the gentiles by means of lamps manufactured in America.'"[236]

Paul's phrase, "such were some of you,"[237] indicates Paul's openness to the potential of hope he could see in others. He knew how God's grace could redirect a life and transform habits. His own experience taught him the humility of receiving God's providences which he understood as undeserved merit.[238]

6. An Optimistic Approach to Life

Christians are full of hope – that's the resurrection principle. Therefore, they do well to enjoy an optimistic

---

[235] Ibid.

[236] Wagner, Peter. op. cit., p. 3.

[237] 1 Corinthians 6:11.

[238] 2 Corinthians 1:12; Ephesians 4:7; 2 Corinthians 12:9.

approach to living. Though the cross was ahead of him, Jesus saw joy in living, even in suffering.[239] With a promise of resurrection in their possession and the example of the Lord in joyfully persevering through his death on the cross, a leader should know that God's *ekklesia* cannot fail. "I will build my church and the gates of Hades will not prevail against it."[240]

John Maxwell reminds his readers of the seemingly impossible conquest of the four-minute mile. It was considered by experts as the four-minute mile barrier. But the medical student Roger Bannister persisted until he ran the mile in less than four minutes. Subsequently, as Maxwell points out,[241] the year after, 37 runners broke the four-minute mile and the year after that, 300 runners broke the four-minute mile. A positive approach to challenges can result in overcoming many of them.

A leader interested in kingdom development needs to focus on the work and words of Jesus, "With God all things are possible."[242] That does not mean God wants all things to happen – which is why a leader needs either personal spiritual discernment or an adjunct who has that gift.

---

[239] Hebrews 12:2.

[240] Matthew 16:18.

[241] Maxwell, John. Developing the Leader in You. p. 106.

[242] Matthew 19:26.

7. A Love Without Strings Attached

Henri J. M. Nouwen wrote that "Our greatest fulfilment lies in giving ourselves to others."[243] God's sacrificial, redemptive love is expressed in the Greek term *agape*. It is love that knows no bounds. It is almost blind in its distinctions. That variety of divine love results in what the Hebrews called *chesed* and the epistles call *grace*.

Grace is love without strings attached, otherwise defined as "God's unmerited favour." Sometimes such grace is defined by its opposite, what Philip Yancey called "ungrace."

> Like a spiritual defect encoded in the family DNA, ungrace gets passed on in an unbroken chain . . . Ungrace does its work quietly and lethally, like a poisonous, undetectable gas. A father dies unforgiven. A mother who once carried a child in her own body does not speak to that child for half a life. The toxin steals on, from generation to generation.[244]

The church which extends love without strings attached is a church that will act in the same manner and with the same love that God endorses. The First Baptist Church of Sioux Falls, South Dakota, resolved, under its pastor Roger Fredrikson, to reach out to alienated youth. The

---

[243] Nouwen, Henri J. M. In Joyful Hope. p. 21.

[244] Yancey, Philip. What's So Amazing About Grace? p. 79.

work became an object lesson in learning how to love without attaching strings to that love. It opened its sanctuary doors 24 hours a day, and then a Firehouse – a drop-in, coffeehouse ministry. Fredrikson told of the downside of disappointment which accompanied the ministry, largely among people who were challenges to love.

> Some of our people who had been with us from the start simply told us in love, "I didn't bargain for this. I've had it. I can't go on." That eager commitment we had at the beginning had worn thin and it seemed like the living centre was being dissipated and coming apart. Even closing up three or four times to regroup didn't change things much.
> Yet every time we seriously faced the possibility of saying, "Our mission is complete; we're going out of business," there were a stubborn few who dug in and insisted that this was no time to quit . . . A committed, gutsy type . . . laid it on the line. "Why do Christians always want to run for the hills when the going gets rough?"[245]

Stephen Covey reminds his readers that love can be a noun or a verb. As a noun it is a subject or an object. As a verb it is active.

> Proactive people make love a verb. Love is something you do, the sacrifices you make, the giving of self, like a mother bringing a newborn into

---

[245] Fredrikson, Roger. God Loves The Dandelions. p. 109.

the world. If you want to study love, study those who sacrifice for others, even for people who offend or do not love in return. If you are a parent, look at the love you have for the children you sacrificed for. Love is a value that is actualized through loving actions. Proactive people subordinate feelings to values. Love, the feeling, can be recaptured.[246]

Grace is no quitter either. Grace does not say, "You change and then I'll love you!" Grace says, "Today, you will be with me in paradise."[247]

8. A Decided Discernment

A leader who wants the Lord to "give the growth," as Paul put it,[248] needs spiritual discernment. He or she requires discernment if choosing associates with appropriate gifts for the mission. He or she requires a sense of God's direction and a sense of detecting false impulses which may lead a congregation into a spiritual cul-de-sac. Paul said it was essential for the believers in Corinth to understand that wisdom comes in two forms, (1) secular and, (2) spiritual. Secular wisdom has its values but also its limitations. Spiritual wisdom understands motives and godliness.

---

[246] Covey, Stephen R. The Seven Habits of Highly Effective People., p. 80.

[247] Luke 23:43.

[248] 1 Corinthians 3:6.

Those who are unspiritual do not receive the gifts from God's Spirit, for they are foolishness to them, and they are unable to understand them because they are spiritually discerned. Those who are spiritual discern all things, and they are themselves subject to no one else's scrutiny.[249]

Stuart Briscoe discovered a lot about life while working in a secular job prior to entering Christian ministry. He managed to learn how secular discernment can also become spiritual discernment. The world *can* teach the spirit of man and vice versa. However, only a person of spiritual discernment can really see how its secular counterpart impacts on his spiritual life.

I remembered something from my days in England as a bank examiner. One of my responsibilities was to identify counterfeit currency. As a young examiner, I felt a little inept, so I asked an older inspector for some clues on how to recognize counterfeits.
"Spend hours and hours handling the real thing," he advised. "The more familiar you are with the genuine article, the more automatically you will recognize the counterfeit."[250]

---

[249] 1 Corinthians 2:15, 15.

[250] Hybels, Bill, Briscoe, Stuart and Robinson, Haddon. <u>Mastering Contemporary Preaching</u>. p. 49.

One way Briscoe applied this principle was in his career choice. The choice became a calling. He described it this way:

> I started preaching and I discovered (1) I could do it, (2) I enjoyed doing it, and (3) people seemed to be blessed as I was doing it. Eventually, the church affirmed my preaching, and I discovered a gifting. And I learned that where there's a gifting, often there's a calling. And over the years that sense of calling has been crystallized.[251]

Not all Spirit-gifted people have such a gift as discernment.[252] If ever such a gift were needed, it would be with someone involved in leadership positions related to helping create God's community of the redeemed.

9. Biblical Competence, Theological Maturity and Understanding

Church growth is fundamentally grounded in biblical directives. A missioner's sense of biblical instruction may determine the success or failure of the mission. No one stumbles upon God's directives. One must be bathed in them to comprehend the basic principles of missiology.

---

[251] Hybels, Bill, Briscoe, Stuart and Robinson, Haddon. op. cit. p. 10.

[252] 1 Corinthians 12:10.

In Donald McGavran's studies he has noted that a biblical approach to church growth is foundational. Notwithstanding the previous criticism of the church growth gurus' failure to recognize kingdom principles,[253] he correctly insists that church growth must be rooted in apostolic models. These must be biblical, evangelical and theological in theory and practice.

> God unquestionably calls individuals to believe on him and be saved, but as soon as they do believe, it is his evident purpose that they be organized into churches and function as churches. It is only in churches that we see the Word of God growing and multiplying. Wherever in the New Testament, people are converted, you see churches being instituted.[254]

10. A Belief in Mission Partnership

"Our journey unfolds as we put God at the centre, live in a community of people who care about him, and find a place where we can be all that we are meant to be." So wrote Bruce Larson.[255]

Such a community must be inclusive, not exclusive.

---

[253] Page 4.

[254] McGavran, Donald and Arn, Win. How to Grow a Church. pp, 21, 22.

[255] Larson, Bruce. Where Will You Be When You Get Where You're Going?, p. 69.

The young church described in Acts 2 quickly became a sharing church. "They ate their bread with glad and generous hearts," wrote Luke.[256] Luke also described his community as caring and responsive to human need. "All who believed were together and had all things in common; they would sell their possessions and goods and distribute the proceeds to all, as any had need."[257] The church of the apostles included the poor and weak as well as the powerful and the strong.

Church is self-defined as a gathered grouping. She gathers for fellowship – *koinonia* – as well as for worship, prayer, instruction and stratagems. She also scatters – but the gathering precedes her reaching out to others. Lyle Schaller insists that no church can boast of its independence because it cannot be other than interdependent. He writes that their growth depends upon it.

> It is good for individual Christians to be a part of a worshiping congregation – a hermit Christian is a contradiction in terms, (b) it is good for congregations to receive new members into their fellowship – they enrich the life and ministry of that congregation, and (c) denominations tend to be healthier, to place a greater emphasis on mission and ministry, to be more open to new ideas, to be more responsive to change, to be less oriented toward institutional survival goals, when they are

---

[256] Acts 2:46.

[257] Acts 2:44, 45.

142

experiencing numerical growth.[258]

Togetherness is the watchword of body life in the church. One reads sections of Ephesians and notes a marked stress on the word "together." Togetherness is the nature of body life. Paul writes of being "joined together,"[259] "built together,"[260] "heirs together,"[261] "members together,"[262] "sharers together,"[263] and "power together."[264] Can there be any doubt that church is a community of unity? It is in this togetherness that Paul sees the growth and uniqueness of the *ekklesia.*

Donald A. McGavran, in answer to a Win Arn question declared that

> It was a unity of purpose to which the early church was totally committed, God's purpose of bringing men to himself . . . This one unifying purpose motivated the apostles and the new Christians. It was shared by everyone who was baptized in the name of

---

[258] Schaller, op. cit., pp. 13, 14.

[259] Ephesians 2:21.

[260] Ephesians 2:22.

[261] Ephesians 3:6.

[262] Ibid.

[263] Ibid.

[264] Ephesians 3:18.

Jesus. We may say that the growth of the church was dependent upon men coming to feel about salvation the way God feels about it, and yielding themselves to God as ready instruments for his will.[265]

God has ordained that his church find her common purpose in the joy of knowing her Saviour, Jesus Christ the Lord. That oneness ensures her common purpose and common direction. In such unity of being the church will grow and prosper as God wills it.

B. Human Qualities

To these 10 spiritual traits which church leadership requires, a variety of other skills are valuable. Herein are listed nine of them. God is the ultimate entrepreneur and entrepreneurial assets complement the spiritual endowments which God provides. God also uses undedicated gifts and people. Note Gallio to Paul and Nebuchadnezzar to Daniel. God obviously used Caesar and his empire to further divine causes and impulses.

1. A Sense of Urgency; A Possession of Patience

We usually are motivated by the importance of what we do. In a sense the church generally has not commanded

---

[265] McGavran, Donald and Arn, Win. op. cit. p. 19.

respect for its offices because they have been deemed to lack importance. Christians ought to be humble but to diminish the importance of the gospel is not humility but heresy.

"We worked night and day," wrote Paul, "while we preached the gospel to you."[266] "We were gentle among you, like a mother caring for her little children. We loved you so much," he said to them, "that we were delighted to share with you not only the gospel but our lives as well."[267]

Paul surely conveyed the importance of his concern for his friends. He had other impulses. Paul sensed the approaching night when he could no longer work.[268] Perhaps he saw the future in which he would be confined to prison. More likely, this sense of urgency was to win as many people to Christ so that they would be saved and ready for the approaching *parousia*.

Salvation and eternal loss are not popular preachments in most contemporary churches because eternal punishment is carefully avoided in church dialogues. Paul seems to be consistent in his theology of salvation and loss. The kingdom will not be inherited by those who reject the gospel of Christ's salvation. "Do you not know that in a race all the runners run, but only one gets the prize?"[269] Paul was

---

[266] 1 Thessalonians 2:9.

[267] 1 Thessalonians 2:7, 8.

[268] Romans 13:11–13.

[269] 1 Corinthians 9:9:24.

highly motivated and clearly saw the eternal consequences of his work. "I have become all things to all men so that by all possible means I might save some."[270]

Archbishop George Carey told how, on the last day before he moved to a new ministry, he visited the church building for a variety of reasons. But he said that the last thing he did in the building that night was to stop and talk, then pray with a man who wanted to know more about the Christian faith. He said, "It was strangely symbolic that the very last thing I did at St. Nicholas' Church was to talk to someone about the Christian faith. But then, that's what it's all about – isn't it?"[271] It seems the Archbishop knew what was important and yet took the time and observed the patience to minister to an inquirer.

2. A Commitment to Conclusions

This writer served as general manager of the condominium board in which he dwells. Every board meeting deals with issues needing resolution. Whether it is cleaning up clutter near the trash disposal or removing oil deposited on the garage cement floor from a "clunker" car owned by a resident, every action must be "signed off." The responsible employee must deal with the issue by signing his

---

[270] 1 Corinthians 9:23.

[271] Carey, George. op. cit., p. 154.

name that the issue is properly concluded.

Pastors and assigned persons delegated to undertake a service for the Lord should be willing to "sign off" that he or she has completed that assignment. One often finds that accountability for a task to be done is never expected by a church board or committee. Perhaps it is the volunteer nature of a church operation that excuses poor management. Perhaps leaders are fearful of chasing members from their churches if they "get after" them for a dereliction of their duties. Perhaps the importance of the assignment in "kingdom" terms has never been clarified to the person delegated to undertake the assignment. John Maxwell points out that

> Time after time, success comes down to sacrifice – willingness to pay the price. The same is true of a winning team. Each member of the team must be willing to sacrifice time and energy to practice and preparation. He must be willing to be held accountable. He must be willing to sacrifice his own desires. He must be willing to give up part of himself for the team's success.[272]

One suspects that "follow up" is a major flaw in church activity. The critical path approach of engineering has something to teach the church that wants to grow. In engineering, plans are set, achievable goals are measured and

---

[272] Maxwell, John C. Developing The Leaders Around You., p. 148.

timetables are carefully obeyed so that each phase of the project comes on stream efficiently and accurately for the subsequent phase. At the end, when the project is completed, the principles "sign off" that they have finished their assignments and are ready for evaluation.

3. An Acceptance of Reality

Stephen Covey proposes that highly effective people are those with a strong sense of reality. Some persons need radical paradigm changes, he argues, in order to face the real world.[273] The real world is based upon lasting principles. He cites Cecil B. de Mille who stated that "It is impossible for us to break the law. We can only break ourselves against the law."[274] In realizing that truth, the individual has taken a new look at reality. We do not break laws; we break ourselves against laws.

It helps a church leader to understand such an issue. Faith invites its followers to see life in a different perspective. Faith people see the angel guards at Samaria[275] that secular people do not even realize are there. Faith welcomes the future; secularism fears the future. God's

---

[273] Covey, Stephen R. The Seven Habits of Highly Effective People., p. 32.

[274] Covey, Stephen R. op. cit., p. 33.

[275] 2 Kings 6:17.

people will grow in attitude and numbers when they begin to act as if the resurrection mattered to them.

4. A Sense of Self-Understanding

A leader who is confused about himself is an unlikely candidate to lead others anywhere but in the wrong direction. Ezra Earl Jones argues that

> "The strong church of tomorrow will be led by a pastor who has been effective in his or her earlier ministry and is challenged by the opportunities presented by a new congregation. The pastor will also be a person who brings stability to the congregation instead of relying upon it for strength"[276]

Would Paul fail the first part of this test but succeed in the second part? He certainly brought his strengths to the churches but admitted to his ample weaknesses. Moreover, Paul sought the comfort, i.e., the strengthening which the churches could offer to him. Nonetheless, Ezra Earl Jones is correct. The pastor must be a spiritually and emotionally secure person whose inner strength is found in his relationship to Christ.

A pastor or lay leader must know himself as fully as he can. It is the only way he can absorb criticism or even

---

[276] Jones, Ezra Earl. Strategies for New Churches., p. 15.

evaluation. Bill Hybels welcomes evaluation and that surely is a mark of his own inner security. He wrote,

> The elders evaluate every message that I preach, and they give me a written response to it within minutes after I complete the message. One elder – our most discerning when it comes to preaching evaluation – collects responses from the other elders, summarizes them, and writes them on the front of a bulletin and gives it to me before I leave.[277]
>
> Such evaluation, especially if it is severely critical, could devastate a preacher. However, in this instance – as it should be in others – the evaluation process is intended to improve a situation, and therefore the preacher's effectiveness. By the elders' vetting their opinions through a discerning elder, the criticisms are muted and the evaluation has more accuracy in it. This kind of evaluation requires a leader's emotional maturity. When it is offered in this way, it is relatively nonthreatening to the leader.

A mature leader invits evaluation. A poor leader refuses it. Of course, the fairness of the evaluation is essential for it to be helpful to anyone.

5. An Ability to Trust One's Instincts

An ability to know ourselves enables us to also trust

---

[277] Hybels, Bill, Briscoe, Stuart and Robinson, Haddon. op. cit. p. 156.

our instincts. Robert Schuller has written that

> I came to the realization that those who think
> negatively simply do not think highly of themselves.
> Every negative thinker I have ever met distrusts
> himself, belittles himself, and downgrades himself.
> This lack of self-worth lies at the root of almost
> every one of our personal problems.[278]

This writer was once assigned to counselling at a Christian camp for "junior highs." We remember the struggle of knowing who we were from our own adolescent years.

We resolved to personally interview every camper under our supervision. We asked where they came from, their family life, their ambitions, their interests and their spiritual relationship with God. We think it helped the campers to discover who they were and to consider their relationship with God.

The decision to undertake this was pure instinct, not laid on by the camp staff. We felt it was the right thing to do.

How gratifying it was, therefore, to read that Ray Bakke did something similar in his parish program in Chicago. He was a new pastor to a congregation that hated the people in its community! It was a productive exercise for the pastor.

---

[278] Schuller, Robert H. Self Love: The Dynamic Force of Success. p. 11.

I took the trouble to get to know the congregation and interviewed each member. Separately, I asked them, "How did you come to know Jesus Christ?" Each person had come to know him in a different way, and none of them during a morning service in the church. Yet they still wanted me to give invitations every Sunday for people to come forward and be saved. They had been conditioned to want something to happen but not to believe that it ever would, and this was reinforced each week when the invitation was given and nobody went forward.[279]

Bakke made no immediate changes. He had the good sense to ask several other questions until the people themselves provided the impetus for change. Nonetheless, his basic instincts were correct in his approach and understanding of the church dynamics.

6. An Appraisal of Others' Strengths and A Willingness to Delegate

"Interdependence is a higher value than independence," wrote Stephen Covey.[280]   Paul called it togetherness as we have seen. But the world also operates on successful team principles and should be no less for the church.

Working in an ecumenical setting Ezra Earl Jones

[279] Bakke, Ray. The Urban Christian., p. 88.

[280] Covey, Stephen R. op. cit. p. 9.

gathered advice and research from several denominational leaders. The quality of pastoral leadership that came forward most often was the pastor's ability to relate with others. That is axiomatic. What follows is a summary of Jones' analysis with some quotations included:

Qualities of effective new church pastors.

1. **Personal religious commitment**, committed to the faith to which he seeks to lead others, with "an evangelistic concern that persons outside the church have the opportunity of participating in the Christian life through the acceptance of Jesus Christ as Lord and Saviour. He must have a faith that demands to be shared."

2. **An understanding of the primary task of pastor**, i.e., be more than a manager of an organization or social institution, but "he must also recognize the priestly role that the pastor alone carries."

3. **Capacity to utilize resources**, i.e., be "adept in evoking the best in people and enabling the early members to do many tasks for which they may not have had prior training or experience."

4. **Good interpersonal relating style**. "In addition to understanding the needs of people, the pastor must have the ability to show appreciation and support for persons as persons. He must be open, accessible, and sensitive to the needs of members and residents of the community."

153

5. **Creativity**. "He will be capable of putting together a blueprint for the church that can be shared with the members and can be tested and modified by the total group until a common vision and common goals are brought forth."[281]

The leader's task is to empower his people to upbuild God's kingdom. Therefore, his or her work is to help others in a way so as to enrich their sense of ministry and ownership in the kingdom's objectives. The early church apostles found they could not do it all themselves and so they delegated the responsibilities to those who had abilities to carry them out.[282] It was a solution to solve the bottleneck of ministry which Moses had discovered from good advice hundreds of years earlier.[283]

Once again, Covey adds positively to this discussion. The opposite of sharing is hoarding and the opposite of delegating is self-centredness. Covey writes,

> Perhaps the most common centre today is the self. The most obvious form is selfishness, which violates the values of most people. But if we look closely at many of the popular approaches to growth and self-fulfilment, we often find self-centring at their core.

---

[281] Jones, Ezra Earl. op cit. p. 110 ff.

[282] Acts 6:4.

[283] Exodus 18:17.

154

There is little security, guidance, wisdom, or power in the limited centre of self. Like the Dead Sea in Israel, it accepts but never gives. It becomes stagnant.[284]

Churches and leaders alike begin to stagnate when they hold onto power for themselves or fail to see the principle of sharing what the kingdom growth requires. There's a question shared which applies to many denominations but I will apply it for my own. The question asks, "How many Baptists does it take to change a light bulb?" The answer comes from the many who hear it. "Change?" "Did someone say, *change?*" Lack of willingness to change can be a form of selfishness which announces the obituary of many congregations. Among the many wars Paul had to fight as a missionary was the combat called "change."

7. A Loyalty of Permanence

Some business practices may tell the church how not to do their work. Loyalty to staff is one of them. Sometimes churches can be more loyal to their staffs than to the benefit of the gospel, not "telling the truth in love"[285] to employees who either are not performing responsibly or are providing

---

[284] Covey, Stephen R. op. cit. p. 118.

[285] Ephesians 4:15.

155

poor direction. Often, especially recently, business has cared little about loyalties to employees while attempting to reach higher profitability. Loyalty is a very important element in congregational life, however. A pastor and people need to share their loyalty with each other. Dependability in stewardship and regular giving is a reflection of faith and grace.

George Barna notes that church shopping reflects a loss of loyalty among Christian people.

> What is missing for most people is a vision that focussed their loyalty. An interesting consequence of vision in vision-led churches is that people are more likely to feel they are truly part of the church. They have a heightened sense of loyalty because the own the vision for ministry. This sharing of a common vision blends people together in a manner that otherwise may not be possible.[286]

The apostle Paul set the bar very high when it comes to loyalty. How he tried to keep contact with his friends! He encouraged them, cajoled them, warned them, showed affection to them – in a word, he was "there" for them. His was a personal commitment to the church and its people that could never be discounted or discarded. Such loyalty uplifts the discouraged and embraces the wayward.

Stephen Covey put it a different way.

---

[286] Barna, George. op. cit., p. 116.

Keeping a commitment or a promise is a major deposit; breaking one is a major withdrawal. In fact, there's probably not a more massive withdrawal than to make a promise that's important to someone and then not come through. The next time a promise is made they won't believe it. People tend to build up their hopes around promises, particularly promises about their basic livelihood.[287]

We may no longer be interested in brand loyalty or even denomination loyalty. In some situations these may only be habits anyway. What matters is that believers be loyal to one another and especially to Christ.

8. Follow-up and Remedial Ministry

Paul excelled at "follow-up." His letters to churches he had once led reflect Paul's habit of tidying up the loose ends of unfinished church business. Since he felt accountable to Christ for his apostolate, he knew he needed to revisit, if not in person, at least in correspondence, unsolved challenges and unresolved tensions.

Such issues exist in every congregation. Hurt feelings, misunderstood words, intolerant opinions, scathing rebuttals find their way into every church fellowship, whether in the grapevine of gossip or the power plays at

---

[287] Covey, Stephen R. op. cit. p. 193.

business meetings.

Conflict resolution activities should always be a part of ongoing organizations. Sales managers call regular meetings. Staff personnel embark on renewal exercises and managers try to rebuild team spirit after some undoing of it. The church is the ideal organism to practise such redemptive activity. It is an organism built on the principle of reconciliation – resolution between God and man, between races and between individuals.[288] Heed Stephen Covey:

> It takes a great deal of character strength to apologize quickly out of one's heart rather than out of pity. A person must possess himself and have a deep sense of security in fundamental principles and values in order to genuinely apologize.[289]

Nonetheless, apologies must be made. It is Christ's way to forgive and be forgiven. The mark of the church is better served by redemptive activity than by theological pronouncements. The sooner a church learns that lesson, the healthier it will be. Moreover, the reconciliation factor is a reflection of the love of Christ in that believing community and it has an attractiveness to outsiders that beckon them to enter the fellowship

---

[288] Ephesians 3:14.

[289] Covey, Stephen R. op. cit. p. 197.

158

9. A Good Measure of Hard Work

Church growth ministry is not for someone suffering from voluntary inertia. Jesus bore a cross and invited his disciples to do the same – daily.[290] The cross is a synonym for sacrifice, of total commitment. Growth requires all the effort leading up to it, as Paul told his people in Corinth, planting and watering the gospel seed.[291]

In one analysis of principles of church growth Lyle Schaller notes that growth won't happen by wishing it. He wrote,

> Despite [a] plethora of creative ideas and programs, the best single approach still is the old-fashioned system of personal visitation. This system affirms the value of face-to-face relationships and requires the pastor and lay volunteers to call, on a regular basis, on individuals and families who do not have any active relationship with any worshiping congregation. Some experienced practitioners of this approach contend that a *minimum* of six visits must be made, perhaps a month or two apart, before any decision can be made on whether or not that person's name should be retained on the list of prospective new members. Experience suggests that ten thousand such calls, some made by the pastor and others by

---

[290] Matthew 16:24.

[291] 1 Corinthians 3:6.

159

carefully trained lay people, will result in one hundred to two hundred new members' uniting with the congregation. If all the calling is done by the pastor and/or a trained parish visitor and is directed at the first residents of new single-family homes, the response rate may be a little higher. If the calling is done entirely by laity who do not live in the community where the church building is, and if there are significant language, racial or socioeconomic class differences between the callers and the persons visited, the response rate may be somewhat lower.

This endorsement of visitation evangelism is offered partly to affirm that approach, but primarily to introduce the first of seven basic assumptions one which the book is based.

The most effective lay volunteers for visitation evangelism come in disproportionately large numbers from among those who have been members for less than three years, and who have joined since the arrival of the present minister . . . A corollary . . . is that there are some pastors who are very interested in church growth, but who are less than enthusiastic about visitation evangelism.[292]

The last comment is the telling one. Many want results without the work involved in achieving results. Bill Hybels argues for delayed gratification.[293] When the work is

---

Schaller, Lyle E. Growing Plans., pp. 9, 10.

Hybels, Bill. Making Life Work. p. 72.

done then there's time to slack off.

Hybels argues that sloth is a serious problem for those who want to make life work. He suggests attending "Ant Academy."[294] Moreover, Ant Academy teaches its observers an attitude of self-starting. He cites the proverb which invites a common slug to watch how ants do their assignments. "Go to the ant, you sluggard. Consider its ways and be wise! It has no commander, no overseer or ruler, yet it stores its provisions in summer and gathers its food in harvest." [295]

Common sense backs up the biblical adage that "what you sow you will also reap."[296] Ministry is hard work and as Jesus said, "No one who puts hand to plough and looks back is fit for service in the kingdom of God."[297]

Summary

Many facts enrich or debase the life of a church and determine its growth potential. Some of these are "common sense" and some are rooted in spiritual maturity. Much church growth depends upon whether the people of God see themselves as an organization or an organism. The former is

---

[294] Hybels, Bill. Making Life Work., p. 38.

[295] Proverbs 6:6–8.

[296] Galatians 6:7.

[297] Luke 9:62.

human; the latter, of God.

The basic principles of church growth rest in the reality that the church is Christ's and that he will require that it conforms to the principles of his kingdom. If growth is to happen, it will be God working through his servant to accomplish God's objectives. Those are basic – to save a lost world, to welcome the lost into his loving fellowship and to give us – his trophies of grace – to one another.

BIBLIOGRAPHY ON CHURCH GROWTH

Books

Bakke, Ray. The Urban Christian. Downers Grove, IL: InterVarsity Press, 1987.

Barna, George. User Friendly Churches. Ventura CA: Regal Books, 1991.

_____. The Power of Vision. Ventura CA: Regal Books, 1992.

Banks, Robert. Paul's Idea of Community. Peabody Mass: Hendrikson Publications Inc., 1994 pp. 233.

Barclay, William. Ambassador for Christ. Valley Forge: Judson Press. 1973, 1975. pp. 183.

Barth, Karl. Prayer and Preaching. London: SCM Press. 1964

Beasley-Murray, G. R. The Broadman Bible Commentary, Vol. 11. 2 Corinthians. Nashville: Broadman Press, 1971. pp. 1–76.

Bentall, Shirley. Discovering the Deep Places. Toronto: The Canadian Baptist, 1988.

163

Bibby, Reginald W., and Posterski, Donald. The Emerging Generation. Toronto: Irwin Publishing, 1985

Brackney, William H. Christian Volunteerism: Theology and Praxis. Grand Rapids MI: Wm. B. Eerdmans Publishing Co., 1997.

Brown, Raymond Bryan. *Broadman Bible Commentary Vol. 10.* Nashville: Broadman Press.1 Corinthians. 1970. pp. 287–397.

Bruce, F. F. The Pauline Circle. Grand Rapids MI: Eerdmans, 1985. pp. 106.
_____. Paul: Apostle of the Heart Set Free. Grand Rapids MI: Eerdmans. 1977. [pp. (510)].

Callahan, Kennon L. Building for Effective Mission. San Francisco: Jossey-Bass Publishers, 1995.

Colson, Charles. A Dangerous Grace. Dallas: Word Books, 1994.

Carey, George. The Church in the Market Place. Harrisburg PA: Morehouse Publishing, 1990.

Covey, Stephen R. The Seven Habits of Highly Effective

People. New York: Simon and Schuster, 1989.

Craig, Clarence T., and Short, John. *The Expositor's Bible, Vol. 10.* The First Epistle to the Corinthians. Nashville: Abingdon Press, 1953. pp. 3–262.

Dobson, Ed. Starting a Seeker Sensitive Service. Grand Rapids MI: Zondervan. 1993.

Easum, William. How To Reach Baby Boomers. Nashville: Abingdon Press, 1991.

_____. Dancing With Dinosaurs. Nashville: Abingdon Press, 1993.

Edwards, David. Good News in Acts. Glasgow: Fontana Books, 1974. pp. 175.

Filson, Floyd V. and Reid, James. *The Interpreter's Bible, Vol. 10.* The Second Epistle to the Corinthians. Nashville: Abingdon Press, 1953. pp. 265–425.

Gager, John C. Kingdom and Community: The Social World of Early Christianity. Englewood Cliffs NJ: Prentice-Hall Inc. 1975. pp. 157.

Geffcken, Johannes. The last days of Graeco-Roman paganism. Amsterdam: North-Holland Publishing Company, 1977. pp. 343.

Grant, Robert M. Early Christianity and Society. New York: Harper & Row, 1977. pp. 221.

Fisher, Fred. Commentary on 1 & 2 Corinthians. Waco: Word Books. 1975. pp. 453.

Fredrikson, Roger. God Loves the Dandelions. Waco: Word Books, 1975.

Harrington, W. Frank. First Comes Faith. Louisville: Geneva Press. 1998.

Hock, Ronald F. The Social Context of Paul's Ministry. Philadelphia: Fortress Press, 1980. pp. 112.

Howard, Fred D. 1. Corinthians: Guidelines for God's People. Nashville: Convention Press. 1983 pp. 140.

Hybels, Bill, Briscoe, Stuart, and Robinson, Haddon. Mastering Contemporary Preaching. Portland OR: Multnomah Press, 1989.

Hybels, Bill. Descending Into Greatness. Grand Rapids MI:

Zondervan. 1993.

_____. The God You're Looking For. Nashville: Thomas Nelson Inc., Publishers. 1997.

_____. Making Life Work. Downers Grove IL: InterVarsity Press., 1998.

Johnson, Sherman E. Paul the Apostle and His Cities. Wilmington Delaware: Michael Glazier Inc., 1987. pp. 186.

Jones, Ezra Earl. Strategies for New Churches. New York: Harper & Row Publishers, 1976.

Jones, E. Stanley. Christian Maturity. Nashville: Abingdon Press, 1957, 1985.

Larson, Bruce. Where Will You Be When You Get Where You're Going? Garden Grove CA: Crystal Cathedral Ministries, 199?.

Luccock, Halford E. In the Minister's Workshop. Nashville: Abingdon Press, 1944.

McGavran, Donald A., with Arn, Win. How To Grow A Church. Glendale CA: Regal Books, 1973, 1978.

Maxwell, John C. Developing The Leader Within You. Nashville: Thomas Nelson Inc., 1993.

_____. Developing The Leaders Around You. Nashville: Thomas Nelson Inc., 1995.

Macgregor, G. H. C. *The Interpreter's Bible, Vol. 9*. The Acts of the Apostles. Nashville: Abingdon Press, 1953. pp. 3–352.

Meeks, Wayne A. The First Urban Christians. New Haven: Yale University Press, 1983. pp. 299.

Nouwen, Henri J. In Joyful Hope. St. Louis: Creative Communications for the Parish. 1997.

Papahatzis, Nicos. Ancient Corinth. Athens: Ekdotike Athenon S. A., 1978. pp. 112.

Percy, Harold. Following Jesus: First Steps on The Way. Toronto: Anglican Book Centre, 1993.

_____. Good News People. Toronto: Anglican Book Centre, 1996.

Posterski, Donald. Reinventing Evangelism. Markham ON: InterVarsity Press., 1989.

Schaller, Lyle E. Growing Plans. Nashville: Abingdon. 1983, 1989.

Schuller, Robert H. Self Love: The Dynamic Force of Success. New York: Hawthorne Books Inc., 1969.

Smith, T. C. *The Broadman Bible Commentary Vol. 10.* Acts. Nashville: Broadman Press, 1970. pp. 1–152.

South, James T. Disciplinary Practices in Paul's Texts. Lewiston NY: The Edwin Mellen Press. 1992. pp. 218.

Stevens, R. Paul and Collins, Phil. The Equipping Pastor. Bethesda MD: The Alban Institute. 1993.

Tolbert, Malcolm O. Layman's Bible Book Commentary, Vol. 22: Philippians, Colossians, 1 & 2 Thessalonians, 1 & 2 Timothy, Titus, Philemon. Nashville: Broadman Press, 1980. pp. 168.

Wagner, Peter. Church Growth and the Whole Gospel. New York: Harper & Row Publishers., 1981.

Yancey, Philip. What's So Amazing About Grace? Grand Rapids MI: Zondervan Publishing House. 1997.

Bibliography on Paul

Babcock, William (ed.). Paul and the Legacies of Paul. Dallas: Southern Methodist University Press. 1990. pp. 426.

Bruce, F. F. Paul: Apostle of the Free Spirit. Exeter: The Paternoster Press. 1977. pp. 491.

Coggan, Donald. Paul: Portrait of a Revolutionary. London: Hodder and Stoughton, 1986. pp. 255.

Johnson, Hubert Rex, Who Then Is Paul? Washington DC: University Press of America. 1980. pp. 249.

Hunter, A. M. The Fifth Evangelist. London: SCM Press, 1980, pp. 136.

Lentz, John Clayton Jr. Luke's Portrait of Paul. Cambridge: Cambridge University Press. 1993. pp. 192.

Murphy-O'Connor, Jerome. Paul: A Critical Life. Oxford: Clarendon Press. 1996. pp. 416.

Ramsay, William M. St. Paul the Traveller and the Roman Citizen. Grand Rapids MI: Baker Publishing House. 1925, reprinted 1980. pp. 464.

Sanders, E. P. Paul. Oxford: Oxford University Press, 1991. pp. 138.

Watson, Francis. Paul, Judaism and the Gentiles. Cambridge:

Cambridge University Press. 1986. pp. 246.

Wedderburn, A. M. (ed.). W. Paul and Jesus: Collected Essays. Sheffield: JSOT Press, 1989. pp. 207.

Journals

Review and Expositor. Vol. LXXX, No. 3, Summer 1983. First Corinthians. pp. 313–425.

The Theological Educator, Vol. XIV, No. 1, Fall 1983. First Corinthians. pp. 10–94.

.

www.ingramcontent.com/pod-product-compliance
Lightning Source LLC
Chambersburg PA
CBHW052052090426
42739CB00010B/2139